THE
GOSPEL
OF
SECRETS

A MEMOIR OF TRUTH, LIBERATION AND LOVE

KENNETH WORTLEY

This Memoir is dedicated to

Marcus Vinicius Pinto Costa,

The one man who taught me that LOVE is still possible in my life.

CONTENTS

Images dedicated to the stories behind the story.

CHAPTER 1

THE ROOTS OF SUPPRESSION

My story is steeped in tradition—shaped by family, guided by faith, and shadowed by silence. This is the memoir of a preacher whose life was defined as much by what was hidden as by what was proclaimed. Why another memoir about a preacher wrestling with his sexuality? Because my story, while deeply personal, is far from unique. It echoes the silent struggles of countless others—teachers, clergy, leaders—whose lives are shaped by expectation, secrecy, and courage.

In sharing this journey, I hope you'll not only hear my story but see the shared weight of living a life that wasn't fully truthful. Living a life that isn't fully truthful consumes immense energy, something I hope you can understand. The effort of maintaining facades and navigating half-truths takes its toll, affecting every aspect of one's existence. Embracing authenticity brings relief and renewal, allowing that energy to be redirected towards living genuinely. The story I share is not just my own; it is a reflection of a shared human experience, one of self-discovery and the liberating power of truth. Growing up in a conservative church, conversations about sexuality were nonexistent. My parents never spoke of it either. Instead, I found a surprising kind of emotional resonance through the smooth, melodic tunes of Barry Manilow. I was captivated by his music—oblivious at first to the man behind the lyrics. Learning later about his sexuality stirred something inside me: curiosity, admiration, and confusion. As you delve into my narrative, I ask for your openness and understanding, inviting you to embrace the oddities and nuances of the decisions I've made. These were choices birthed from a world starkly different from today's increasingly accepting communities. My story is a chronicle of growing through silence, overcoming suppression, and finding peace and authenticity.

This memoir uncovers the journey of my life, shaped by the secrets I kept and the courage it took to finally step into the light. Let this be a testament to transformation and the profound liberation that comes with embracing one's truth. From a young age, I was ingrained with the belief that masculinity was the cornerstone of a man's identity. "Men were men," they said in my household; anything less was met with skepticism and ridicule. This rigid expectation wove through every aspect of my life—whether idolizing sports figures who never dared to show vulnerability or criticizing entertainers like Liberace and Freddie Mercury as anomalies. Yet, as a paradox began to form within me, a secret admiration and a challenge to these norms nudged at my consciousness. In a realm where athletic prowess was a pillar of acceptance, the notion of an athlete expressing their true self, let alone their sexuality, felt as unimaginable as snow in July. However, as my world expanded, narratives began to unravel, tugging at the strict boundaries I was taught. As these contradictions surfaced, they illuminated the complexity of who I was becoming—how I fit, and yet did not fit, into the neat categories that had defined my history. This memoir accompanies you through the complexity of learning and unlearning, accepting, and redefining masculinity and identity from this lens. Through my story, I hope to shed light on the universal struggle for self-acceptance amid societal expectations.

My story is not just a reflection of where I come from but a piece of the larger fabric of change, exploring how a culture steeped in traditional values confronts the evolving notions of identity and acceptance. In Michigan, General Motors wasn't just an employer— it was a cultural force. Working for GM meant status and security, especially for young men like my own brother.

I was expected to follow that path too, trading dreams for factory assembly lines, and manhood for machinery. Masculinity was measured in hours worked and mainly steering gears built for factories all over the state. This was a place where cars weren't just vehicles; they were symbols of the American Dream, promising prosperity powered by assembly lines and unabating ambition. The GM ethos quietly echoed throughout our home, influencing everything from our evening conversations to the heroes we idolized on and off the field. Yet amidst this framework, I sensed that the engine of change was quietly rumbling beneath the surface, poised to challenge the traditions set before me. It was a time of transformation, where personal truth began to veer defiantly against the established norms. My place in the family felt cemented as the youngest, the observer of these exchanges. Watching my older brother lean in during such stories, I saw a deep bond form, molded by shared interests in the gritty tales of battle. Meanwhile, I found myself more a spectator than a participant in these rituals, shaping my understanding of a father whose affection was quietly demonstrated through action rather than touch. Although it may be conceived that I am being critical of my upbringing, it's crucial to recognize that my parents did their best during the turbulent '60s. Their love and efforts were unwavering, and I deeply love and value them, placing no blame on how they shaped my views on life.

While World War II was woven into the fabric of my father's life, his home was a sanctuary where emotional complexities were tucked away, replaced by a resolve to build a family—a quintessentially American pursuit. My mother, too, played her part with grace, supporting the household while nurturing our lives. Reflecting on my upbringing, my mother was one of the few women in our community who chose to work full-time outside the home—a quiet act of strength that shaped my view of resilience in a different way. Despite an emotional distance, my parents managed our household with steadfast dedication, providing a supportive environment filled with love and aspirations for their sons. It's this silent strength, shared by parents who endured life's adversities without much overt display of affection, that shaped my journey and instilled in me the values of resilience and hard work. In this tapestry, where masculinity and resilience were prized above all, the echoes of artillery were as familiar as the morning radio. My father's legacy—etched in both the glow of the past and the glass of coffee cups—taught me the quiet power of steadfastness amidst life's noise. In the turbulence of the 1960s, as the world seemed to spin faster than our little middle-class family could catch up, I found my anchor within the hallowed halls of our church. Our lives, deeply rooted in religious practice, revolved around the church community—a seamless extension of my family. From the tenor of hymnals echoing each Sunday morning to the various church activities that stitched together my week, I discovered a place where my budding identity could bloom. It was the church that shaped my earliest dreams, where visions of leading a congregation, of becoming a pastor, first took root. In those sacred pews, I dreamed big, imagining myself as the leader of my own church, guiding others through the scriptures, modeling truth, and living an authentic life for others. One can see the pressure I was under to live a truth-filled life as a leader. Despite my family's lukewarm appreciation for formal education, I was steadfast. I began to explore colleges and seminaries that resonated with my aspirations, readying myself for a path less valued in our household. I yearned to learn, to preach, and to lead— steps toward a destiny that seemed divinely guided. This resolve sprouted not from rebellion but from a deep, abiding faith that wove through every fiber of my being. I was determined to see it through, believing that my journey to pastoral leadership was as much about personal growth as it was about spiritual servitude.

In the hushed shadows of adolescence, I stood at a crossroads where understood norms began to blur. Growing up, I found myself inexplicably detached from the typical pursuits of teenage romance—an absence of attraction toward girls that seemed just another anomaly in the mosaic of my youth, a facet of my life that begged to be silenced in shame and deep, deep denial. During my teenage years, I rarely dated girls. I might go out on special occasions at school, but romance always felt like a script I was supposed to follow—not something I naturally desired. Ironically, I had many close friendships with girls, but I struggled to connect with boys in the same way. Relationships with them felt more distant and more fragile. Perhaps I should have known, or perhaps my heart knew long before my mind dared to acknowledge. In the dimly lit confines of my garage, a pivotal moment began to take shape. My two neighborhood friends and I gathered around a bundle of magazines, their pages alive with forbidden allure. As their eyes fixated on the alluring images of women, I found myself, almost involuntarily, drawn to the images of the men depicted. This realization, surfacing from a place deep within, stirred a profound conflict in me. Here, in silence, the layers of my identity began to unravel, introducing a complexity I had yet to fully understand. For them, these porn pictures ignited curious excitement. For me, it only marked a revelation I wasn't ready to accept—a disinterest in the women depicted, replaced by a quiet, undeniable curiosity about the men. Perhaps that day was a turning point—not because of what we looked at, but because of what it revealed. My disinterest in the women, my quiet fixation on the naked men...it was all there, waiting to be acknowledged, but I wasn't ready. I buried that truth as deeply as I could, convinced it had no place in the life I was meant to lead.

My growing realization wasn't signaled by signs or threads but by a persistent, gentle pull— a call to recognize a truth I struggled to keep buried beneath layers of denial. Each hint of this truth presented itself as both subtle and compelling, a quiet acknowledgment of a reality I often tried to suppress. I labored intensely to submerge these desires under a guise of normalcy, hoping they would remain hidden from a world not yet ready for my truth or for me to claim it. My deepest fears whispered that I was different, a difference that rested uneasily alongside my church teachings and conservative upbringing. The chasm between what I felt and what I was taught to believe seemed insurmountable at the time, a silent barrier I could only cross in the privacy of my thoughts. Yet, even then, the light of understanding began to seep through, revealing the complex tapestry of identity that I would one day embrace. At all costs, I lived a life of denial and secrets.

Returning to the sanctuary of religion only amplified my feelings of guilt, as I grappled with an internal conflict between innate desires and learned beliefs. Steeped in a culture where the church held sway over minds and morals, I was taught that my unasked-for feelings were sinful—a breach of the pious fabric of my upbringing. In my theology, God could not create gay people; He doesn't make mistakes in His creation. Growing up in a web of evangelical doctrines, my world was divided starkly between expectations and reality. The teachings I received left little room for deviation from traditional narratives about identity and love. Such institutions entrenched within families often leave individuals in a state of internal dissonance, which I certainly felt during these formative years. In navigating this labyrinth of conflicting identities and beliefs, I found myself reaching for understanding and acceptance—a journey not easily traveled in such a stringent environment. Understanding how these contradictions tied my identity back into the threads of community and faith has been crucial. Although difficult, this tension was transformative, ultimately granting me the clarity to reconcile faith with personal truth.

In the silenced corridors of my upbringing, where heaven's Choirs were thought to echo. I wrestled with the hidden parts of myself that my church, with all its fiery sermons and communal prayers, urged me to bury. Growing up in a deeply religious evangelical Baptist environment embedded in conservative values, I was constantly ensnared by teachings that held traditional sexual norms as sacrosanct. The perceived sanctity inside these walls was a double-edged sword—intended for salvation, yet often leading instead to shadows of guilt and shame about who I truly was. This was a world where deviation from the prescribed path was a lonely venture, fraught with the heavy burden of secrecy. Echoes of sermons on morality and sin were ever-present reminders, pitting my identity against the doctrine. To acknowledge my attractions, my truth, seemed akin to crossing an unbreachable divide. The tension was palpable, magnified by the constant teachings that deemed my feelings an abomination—a conflict as impactful as it was internal.

Such environments, prevalent in many churches, can extend these pressures universally. They compel individuals into lives shadowed by denial and inner turmoil, ingraining the belief that there is no reconciliation between faith and self. Yet, understanding these dynamics is pivotal in the journey toward self-discovery and acceptance. Embracing one's identity while maintaining one's faith may seem paradoxical, but it holds the promise of transformation, paving a road to genuine reconciliation with one's true self. Growing up in a tight-knit family where the annual deer hunt was a sacred ritual, there was an implicit expectation to partake in the tradition—an expectation that manifested as a rifle under the Christmas tree, a gift that was less a present and more a rite of passage into the fraternity of masculinity. I didn't know what to think when my father presented me with a rifle; it was meant as a rite of passage into the world of family hunting—a token binding me to allegiance with my father and brother. On the day of the hunt, my brother led me into the wild heart of Michigan's woods, positioning me with precision under the protective canopy of a bluff. His voice echoed sternly in my ear, "Don't forget to only shoot deer with horns," as he vanished into the underbrush, leaving me alone with my thoughts. At the sharp crack of dawn, it brought with it an initiation, one that I met with more anxiety than anticipation. The darkness of early morning unraveled slowly, giving way to the sound of distant gunfire— a chorus of hunters that marked the opening of the season. The symphony of shots only heightened my nerves, prickling at my consciousness with the underlying fear of friendly fire. Ducking instinctively, I suddenly became aware of a majestic creature emerging through the morning mist. A horned deer stood less than fifteen feet away, its beauty almost rendering time to a standstill. The deer was beautiful as it stood and watched me. I did what was expected. I raised my rifle, aimed, and fired. My brother cheered. My father beamed, but inside I felt nothing. The deer was more than a rite of passage—it was a metaphor for the life I was tepping into; one where expectation often overruled emotion, where appearances mattered more than what lived quietly inside me. I watched the deer fall, my trophy claimed, but felt no victory. Instead, there was a void—a realization wrapped in silence as I kept myself from inspecting what I had done. My brother arrived moments later, his exuberant praise clashing against my silent reflection. As he lifted the deer's head and celebrated, I was chastened by the incomprehensible weight of fulfillment versus expectation—standing amidst the echoes of a choice I had made.

The realization struck me as I stood frozen, the crisp air of the forest wrapping around me like a shroud. My eyes remained fixed on the fallen deer, a stark symbol of the conflict swirling within me. This act, a rite of passage celebrated by my family, left me hollow instead of fulfilled—a silent rebellion against the traditional molds of masculinity I had been expected to embrace. As my brother's joyous shouts echoed through the woods, proclaiming my so-called triumph, I felt a profound dissonance between this enforced ideal and my inner truth. The applause for my beginner's luck only deepened the chasm between the rugged expectations of manhood and the tender spirit I recognized within myself. In that awakening, a seed of self-determination was planted, beginning the journey toward a masculinity that reflected my true self, not just a cultural construct.

It was never meant for me—an understanding that transcended words. Yet they chose to commemorate my apparent success by mounting the deer's head, an offering for storytelling that felt more like a misplaced artifact than a tribute. Time and neglect saw it hang in my garage—a constant taunt of who I wasn't—until one day, gravity took over, and it shattered into irretrievable pieces. Each fragment that clattered to the floor was like an echo liberating me from the lingering shadows of expectations unmet, leaving behind only a lesson about identity found in what is refused, not in what's imposed. My faith, once unchallenged, became a battleground for my soul's awakening. Deep within, I realized that my identity and spirituality could coexist. Embracing both brought not only acceptance but also a profound sense of peace, leading me towards authenticity. Raised in the heart of evangelical teachings, I lived under the shadow of expectations that sometimes felt as rigid as the pews I sat in every Sunday. These lessons echoed with a singular notion: that heterosexuality was the fixed norm. As I matured, I found myself in a conflict with these teachings, feeling the weight of these doctrines clash against my evolving identity. It was like living two lives—outwardly conforming to the comfortable cadence of conformity, while internally dealing with a storm of doubt and longing.

I had long feared it was unattainable. Through this memoir, I lay bare the transformative journey of reconciling faith with my essence—a story not just of struggle, but of hope and eventual triumph in finding one's truth amid profound silence. Evangelical teachings left little room for difference. Heterosexuality was presented not just as a norm, but as the divine design. It was Adam and Eve and not Adam and Steve. Anything else was sin—an error, a flaw, a failing. These teachings were etched into me early, making it nearly impossible to accept what I was beginning to feel. The conflict between faith and identity was a daily storm inside me. But even then, a small voice—persistent and gentle—kept asking, what if you're not broken? What if you were made this way on purpose?

I was raised to believe there was only one path—and I walked it, faithfully and silently. But deep down, I knew I was walking in shoes that didn't quite fit. In the quiet of my upbringing, where prayers filled the air and conformity filled the pews, I began a different kind of spiritual journey: one toward authenticity. Reconciling faith with identity would not come easily. But even in those early years, I could feel something. Shifting—an inner truth beginning to rise, no longer content to be buried beneath tradition and fear.

CHAPTER 2

THE MASK OF MARRIAGE

It's a harsh reality when what appears to be a joyous relationship is merely a mask for existence. The main reason I sought marriage was to fulfill the image of a successful pastor and perhaps curb my homosexual tendencies. The mid-70s marked a turning point in my life. I found myself stepping into a world brimming with promise and the thrill of the unknown. Philadelphia became my new frontier, a city alive with the energy of potential—a place ready to shape dreams yet formed. Nestled just beyond its bustling heart was a small liberal arts college, both daunting and exhilarating. This was my gateway to a larger destiny, one that whispered ancient wisdom and possibilities, inviting me to discover more than I had ever imagined. With this move, I embraced the beginning of a transformative journey, poised on the cusp of self-discovery and boundless aspirations.

From the outset, my aspirations were guided by the dual aims of faith and family. In my heart, I knew that to truly embody the role of being a pastor, I needed more than just personal understanding of these dual roles. Yet, the pressure of finding a partner who would complement this path of spiritual growth weighed heavily on me; I needed a partner who amplified and complemented my vision. The expectation of finding a wife who could fulfill the esteemed role of a pastor's wife—gracious under the spotlight and firm in faith— rested heavily on my shoulders. The pursuit of my calling as a pastor wasn't just about finding the right partner; it was also about meeting the expectations set for me by the congregation and myself. Each class, sermon, and earnest discussion with peers was a step toward my goals, yet the looming pressure cast shadows on every relationship I initiated. The tug-of-war between fulfilling faith-based roles and nurturing a personal relationship added layers of complexity and expectation to my journey.

While navigating academic corridors and foundational theology, the underlying pressure to forge a life that fit the mold was ever present. It was a delicate balance—between pursuing personal truth and meeting the anticipated standards set forth by tradition and community.

Philadelphia became more than a setting; it was a crucible for exploring and shaping my identity, driving me forward on the nuanced paths laid out by hope, faith, and societal expectation. This narrative reflects my personal journey, incorporating elements of expectation and self-discovery, with a focus on the pressures and introspections involved in pursuing a calling while embracing external expectations.

I still dealt with suppressed feelings but honestly believed that marriage and children would bring healing to my inner conflicts. I felt as though an immense weight settled over my soul, urging me into a mold I had never asked to fill. The pressure to conform to the traditional norms of the time was suffocating, each expectation a link in a chain of invisibilities that tethered me to a life that wasn't quite my own. In the eyes of my peers and the church community, aligning my life to fit seamlessly into the ideals of pastoral leadership meant pursuing a marriage that adhered strictly to religious expectations, often at the expense of exploring my own deeper truths. It was as if I navigated life with a shadow over my intentions, perpetually divided between who I was and who I was expected to be.

In my mind, marriage would be a pathway to begin correcting my homosexual tendencies. Fear drove me to this crucial decision, as I worried that my entering the ministry would be seen as hiding my sexuality. The reality I feared was rejection from the faith community if I were a single pastor and the increased likelihood of suspicion, which back then was compounded by a less attractive job resume. If I remained single, all my potential clergy years would be overshadowed by the thoughts of "maybe the pastor is homosexual." I even remembered one church interview asking me if I planned on getting married. They explained that in California, there were so many homosexuals trying to be pastors, and they could not allow that in their local congregation. Choosing marriage would be a way to curb any same-sex attractions and reduce internal conflict and emotional turmoil.

It was 1975 in the First Baptist Church of Michigan where we were married. She was a very attractive young woman raised by a large Italian Catholic family, a family of six. When my wife and I decided to marry, our differing religious backgrounds posed a significant challenge. As a Protestant, concerns about her Catholic upbringing, such as the veneration of saints and the role of Mary, left me uneasy. Many Protestants at the time doubted the notion of Catholics being "born again" in the spiritual sense familiar to evangelical circles. Motivated by a desire for religious unity, I encouraged her to be rebaptized into the Baptist faith. The path was fraught with complexities, but it laid the groundwork for addressing broader spiritual and personal intersections in our marriage.

Our wedding was everything it should have been on the surface—large, joyful, and full of celebration. Family and friends gathered in excitement, and the night echoed with music, laughter, and dancing. But beneath the cheer, I felt something tightening in my chest. As the reception swirled around me, a quiet dread settled in. I smiled for the camera, shook hands, hugged relatives, and accepted well wishes, all the while feeling like I was stepping into a role I didn't fully understand, let alone desire.

As I was about to embark on the journey of married life, nestled beneath the surface excitement was an overwhelming reluctance—a fear rooted deep within the realms of intimacy. The honeymoon, traditionally a time of closeness and discovery, loomed like an insurmountable peak I was expected to scale without fear. But the truth was far from those expectations. The thought of sharing a bed with her, of engaging in the conjugal intimacy that marriage presupposed, stirred more anxiety than anticipation within me. This foreboding didn't stem from the union itself but from reservations left unspoken. I was

reluctant, perhaps even afraid, to engage in the physical act of closeness, especially when guided by a script I couldn't feel truly part of. It wasn't merely the idea of intimacy with a woman that intimidated me; it was the distance between societal norms and the muted whispers of my own truths—a chasm that left me feeling adrift amid my own life's major celebration.

My wife poured herself into her business career. She was the primary provider during my years in college and seminary and even supported our family through financial struggles when I was serving smaller churches. We functioned well as a team—two people committed to a shared life, working side by side—but our physical intimacy faded quietly over time, replaced by a rhythm of companionship and respect. We didn't talk about the lack of intimacy. We existed within it, each of us finding comfort in routine rather than closeness. Evenings slipped into routines, marked by months where closeness never evolved beyond the surface. We functioned together yet missed the spark, the effortless spontaneity that often defines intimacy. For me, engaging in anything more intimate felt awkward, a choreography I had never fully learned.

Over time, her busy life contributed to a widening emotional distance between us. Our intimacy dwindled, but the silence wasn't just a pause in conversation; it symbolized the comfortable yet distant space we occupied—a marriage more aligned with friendship than with passion. We shared life's daily routines side by side, but an essential element was missing—something profound that I dared not acknowledge yet felt keenly in every quiet moment we drifted further apart. Although I am sure she would have welcomed a discussion on how to meet each other's physical needs, I would never broach the subject of how to bring pleasure, a conversation left untouched by both our tongues and minds. While I navigated the awkwardness, unsure of the true mechanics expected from me, our connection remained yet reserved from the uncharted territories of satisfaction and discovery. Beneath the everyday rhythm of life, an undercurrent of unspoken truths persisted—a reminder of how far apart we'd drifted despite our shared lives.

In our relationship, marked by mutual respect and companionship, something vital had slipped away, leaving a void that silent moments only amplified. Paths were left untrodden, questions unvoiced, possibilities unexplored—a testament to the shared atmosphere of profound companionship overshadowed by echoes of silence between us.

Over time, an unsettling truth surfaced—I wasn't truly interested in exploring my wife's physical being. Deep down, this realization bore no resemblance to fading desires; instead, it revealed a truth I had long struggled to acknowledge. Early in our marriage, I became aware of a secret I needed to guard, even as I aimed to provide her with love and companionship. The weight of this secret bore heavily on my soul, and in striving to to maintain this delicate balance, I realized the lengths to which I would go to preserve the facade of our union. Through this journey, I discovered the challenges of living authentically, caught between the roles I played and the person I was meant to be.

As our careers progressed, the quiet anticipation of parenthood began to shadow our conversations.

BECOMING PARENTS

After nine years of marriage, the unspoken expectation of starting a family became a defining force between us. We agreed it was time to have children, and with that decision, the urgency to conceive became palpable. My wife stopped taking birth control— something that had been as routine as our daily lives. This marked a significant turning point, threading the next chapter of our lives with both expectation and resolve to embrace early parenthood together.

It didn't seem long before the news of her pregnancy blossomed into our lives, infusing us with a renewed sense of hope and possibility. I felt joy—real joy, free from internal conflict or fear. It was a moment that transcended any social expectations, marked instead by an

excitement that resonated deeply within as we anticipated the joys and discoveries that awaited us on this new journey together. Our firstborn son graced us with his arrival in California, bringing an extraordinary joy that rippled through the entire family. There was a universal delight that seemed to affirm the life path I'd embarked upon, dispelling any shadow of doubt others might have harbored about my identity. My extended family, once wrapped in speculation, now embraced us with renewed pride as grandparents traveled eagerly to visit and celebrate his presence. This new chapter filled our lives with a sense of fulfillment, weaving threads of closeness that warmed our hearts with every visit.

STRUGGLES AND MIRACLES

Our journey into parenthood wasn't without difficulty. After experiencing three heartbreaking miscarriages, we held our breath through every moment of the next pregnancy. In Spokane, against all odds, our second son was born six weeks early, weighing just 4 lbs. He was a miracle baby. Today, he stands 6'7" tall, strong, and healthy—proof that hope sometimes arrives in the most fragile forms. The notion of welcoming another child into our lives filled us with hopeful anticipation, a shared dream that painted vivid images of a bustling, love-filled home. The transition into parenthood signaled another chapter, yet beneath it lay a lingering nervousness—a fear unspoken, softly tethered to the acknowledgment of truths yet to face. How we would move forward in this woven tapestry of choices—those moments would define us both as parents and as individuals on a journey of undiscovered truths.

What was amazing was our deepening bond. We were good parents. We had a good life together. We were best friends. It wasn't long after the desire to add to the family arose that challenges emerged, for the path ahead promised to be difficult for her.

During this pregnancy, the usual glow was tempered by hurdles and complexities, casting a shadow over what should have been a joyous time. Determined as ever, we faced each obstacle together, fortified by the hope that in the end, our family would be complete. With each passing day, we navigated the ordeal with unwavering faith and resilience, clinging tightly to the belief that brighter days lay ahead and that our growing family would emerge stronger and closer than before.

After enduring the heartbreak of three painful pregnancy losses, each more agonizing than the last, we faced this new chapter with cautious hope shadowed by apprehension. Her doctors, determined and diligent, prescribed a regimen of medications intended to nurture the delicate beginning of new life within her. Each pill represented a beacon of hope, a strategy to ensure this pregnancy would hold, yet it was accompanied by the weight of anxiety and the memory of past heartaches. In time, our journey led us to Spokane—a place filled with promise and the chance for renewal. Amidst all the uncertainty, we clung tightly to each other and the belief that perseverance would lead us to the joy we longed for—a family complete with the laughter and cries of a newborn. This was a crossroad in our lives, marked by resilience and the unwavering hope that light would soon break through the shadowed canopy of our struggles.

The doctor's advice reverberated through the stillness of the examination room like an unexpected toll of finality. They told us that this would be the end of our desire to have any more children—a moment marked not just by medical certainty but also by a weighted silence. It was a decision reluctantly accepted, yet underscored by gratitude for the children and memories we had cherished along the way. The path we had walked to this point was fraught with challenges, yet it had also taught us resilience and the profound depth of love—an undying legacy that would continue to shape our family's future.

Despite our emotional distance, we found deep joy in raising our children. Parenthood became the common ground where our connection thrived. It didn't erase the silence in other areas, but it filled our home with laughter, purpose, and love. Parenting is a joy! Throughout our marriage, I often wondered about the absence of fulfillment from outside sources for her unmet needs. Despite a lack of physical intimacy, something unique blossomed between us—a bond based more on companionship and shared experiences. Our lives intertwined not through conventional intimacy but through profound mutual respect and emotional connection. Together, we crafted a life marked by the deep friendship that proved love can thrive in varied and unexpected forms.

With our family now complete, my heart filled with an overwhelming sense of joy and gratitude. The moment our son was born, a new chapter unfolded—a vibrant tapestry of shared laughter and learning that family life brings. Shifting my focus to fatherhood brought a purpose unparalleled by any role I had known. Our marriage thrived in the realms of friendship and mutual respect. United by shared goals and dreams, we navigated life's tapestry hand in hand. Although the physical intimacy typically expected in a marriage eluded us, our bond was unique and profound—a companionship that filled our days with warmth and contentment.

Being a dad meant embarking on daily adventures filled with little discoveries alongside my son. Each step he took mirrored my own journey, painting a vivid tapestry of exploration and love. These moments, woven into the fabric of family life, brought me immense fulfillment.

Our home resonated with the harmony of shared experiences, where love, trust, and camaraderie played their parts beautifully.

One Sunday morning, standing at the pulpit, a heartwarming yet humorous scene unfolded. My son innocently stood beside me, mimicking my sermon moves. It was both embarrassing and touching, transforming an ordinary day into a cherished memory. The congregation's laughter embraced us, and I felt a rush of pride and love for the little boy who had unknowingly stolen the spotlight. This moment captured the essence of parenthood—a delicate dance of love interwoven with unexpected joys and shared laughter.

Being a pastor comes with the immense responsibility of being the spiritual cornerstone of that local faith community—a luminous beacon of righteousness and exemplar of ideal living. On the surface, my life mirrored this image with almost near-perfection. On the outside, I was everything a pastor was expected to be—a loving father, a faithful husband, a respected spiritual guide. My family looked whole, and from the pulpit, I delivered messages of truth and righteousness. But behind the scenes, I carefully guarded a different truth. I crafted sermons while silently struggling with my own identity. I led prayers every Sunday morning during worship while quietly questioning my place. My life was a masterclass in concealment, a reflection not of dishonesty but of survival. The polished exterior I presented was a shield—not against the world, but against the pain of being rejected by it. And with great difficulty and pain, it worked—until the silence grew too heavy to bear.

Over time, I realized how small lies, large lies, and telling lies in general became ingrained in my daily existence. These falsehoods shielded the deeper truths of my identity. The energy spent upholding this facade hindered me from forming authentic connections. I really didn't know how to connect in a genuine way. This chapter unravels the tension between the facade I presented and the truths I grappled with—a haven of sorts that nudged me toward self-acceptance and authenticity. Recently, reading "The Lies We Tell Ourselves" by Jon Fredrickson gave me insight into why we cling to falsehoods to escape pain. The book describes how these fantasies, rather than easing pain, often lead to greater suffering. This lesson has been illuminating, revealing not only the toll these lies took but highlighting the freedom that comes from embracing one's true self.

CHAPTER 3

THE CALL BEYOND TRADITION

Shortly after the wedding, in the summer of 1972, we embarked on a new chapter as we packed up the pieces of our Michigan life into a rented trailer and set our sights on the unexplored. This was like navigating a bittersweet symphony of emotions. I wasn't just leaving a place; I was leaving behind assumptions, roles, and a silence that had shaped my life for years. My destination lay in a small liberal arts college in the quaint town of St. Davids, nestled just outside the bustling life of Philadelphia. This move felt like a quiet rebellion cloaked in academic ambition—a chance to start untangling who I was from who I had been told I had to be. As I embarked on this new journey, leaving behind the comfort of everything familiar, I knew I was stepping away from home and into a world filled with untapped potential. The shift was both overwhelming and exhilarating. Here I stood at the doorstep of a small liberal arts college in St. Davids, just 35 miles outside Philadelphia—a vibrant tapestry waiting to embrace the diverse threads of possibility that lay ahead. This college community, tight-knit and brimming with varied backgrounds, became my canvas of transformation. It was a place where each interaction and every experience painted a clearer picture of who I was beyond the rigid landscapes of my past. As I prepared to immerse myself in this new environment, the stakes were deeply personal. This was more than just an academic journey; it was a step into self-discovery, a quest to uncover the layers of my identity and redefine my place in a broader world. Here, I would learn to balance newfound freedom with the realities of personal growth, setting the stage for the rich tapestry of experiences that define this pivotal chapter in my life. It was here that I began to unearth parts of myself I had yet to fully understand, eagerly anticipating the personal revelations that awaited. In those formative years, few students bore the title of "married," and the campus adjusted as best it could, allotting us two separate dorm rooms instead of the cozy, solitary married housing that was yet a dream.

My academic pursuits led me through winding paths of sociology, where even the textbooks became mirrors. I remember a lecture on systemic inequity that left me reeling— it challenged my understanding of justice and faith, and I began to wonder how many other truths I had taken for granted. These moments unraveled my certainty and rewove it into something deeper, more personal. The lectures and discussions opened my eyes to the significance of social justice intertwined with faith, dramatically shifting the principles I once considered untouchable. As I stood at the crossroads of academia and spirituality, I embraced the transformation, recognizing how deeply it reshaped my identity and beliefs. Now I want to change the world!

As I stood on the brink of transformation, my evangelical past collided with a missing piece—the call for social justice. Growing up, changing the world wasn't my priority; the teachings I followed focused inward. However, at Eastern, the Department of Sociology challenged everything I thought I knew. The discussions and lessons there expanded my understanding, intertwining social justice with faith. This revelation brought an exhilarating shift. I realized I could channel this newfound perspective into serving my community. By weaving themes of compassion for the sick and support for the downtrodden into my messages, it became my mission to transform the institutional church from within—driven by a passion to manifest change. My life and ministry would become conduits for advocating justice and equity, igniting a fire ready to inspire and rebuild faith with broader, deeper roots. In my church upbringing, there was a stark absence of social justice content; focus was largely on individualistic faith with little emphasis on changing the world. What captivated me most were the teachings of Jesus of Nazareth, who stood as a champion of the outcast and a friend to those who didn't fit societal norms. This perspective resonated deeply with me, reflecting how I felt about my own life. As I embarked on my academic journey, this new understanding intertwined with my faith, challenging me to see the broader implications of religion in everyday life and community. With each graduating hue that accompanied my honors, I moved forward, diving deeper into the sacred texts and mysteries of theology. Pursuing a Master's Degree in Theological Studies, I pored over dense lines of Greek and Hebrew, the languages of divinity.

After graduating with a Bachelor's degree in Sociology, I set my sights on seminary in the city of Philadelphia. During my seminary years, I was surrounded by brilliant theologians, all grappling with the challenge of balancing personal faith with broader societal needs. The mission of the seminary was captivating: "the whole gospel for the whole world." This vision resonated deeply with me, igniting a desire to embrace a holistic faith that addressed not only spiritual but also social concerns. I aspired to bring this comprehensive understanding to the world I would serve, striving to incorporate social justice into my sermons. Although there was a prevalent silence on LGBTQ+ issues, the overarching mission empowered me to approach my faith with renewed vigor and inclusivity. This was the beginning of my journey to redefine the impact of faith in my own life and the lives of those I would encounter.

After graduation, I accepted my first pastoral call—a congregation nestled in the small picturesque town of Canon City. With my wife and our sense of purpose, we moved west. That call became the first step in what would be a decades-long journey through pastoral ministry: from Colorado to the lush outskirts of Portland, then the suburban stretches of Walnut Creek, and finally to the inland northwest of Spokane, Washington. Each place brought new faces and new versions of me. The sermons changed. The silence did not. My

The role as pastor deepened, but so did the emotional distance in my relationship with my wife, and the quiet conflict building within myself.

Our next move was to Spokane, Washington, where I would serve my last church. This city became the stage for a profound transformation in my life. Here, amidst the familiar and the novel, I found a place to contemplate my past while preparing to face the changes ahead. Spokane would not only shape my closing chapter in ministry but also become the backdrop for the significant personal changes that awaited me. Each location added a brushstroke to the evolving portrait of my life, teetering between who I was expected to be and who I was becoming.

As a pastor, I was expected to embody moral clarity and spiritual strength. To many, I did. My messages on Sunday mornings were heartfelt, my family appeared whole, and I was praised for the way I made scriptures come alive and feel personal. But beneath the accolades, the church also became a hiding place. A structured world where expectations gave me a script to follow, even if I didn't reflect the full truth of who I was. I wore the robe of righteousness well, but inside, I was still in conflict with doubts, with secrets, and with the growing need to be honest with myself. Throughout my years of ministry, I've come to recognize that the institutional church served both as a platform for my passionate pursuit of social justice and a sanctuary where I could hide from the complexities of my own reality. While my sermons sought to address the needs of the oppressed, many congregants yearned for traditional messages focusing more on personal salvation and altar calls. These divergent expectations often led to conflicts within the church. Francis of Assisi's call to "comfort the afflicted and afflict the comfortable" resonates with me, underscoring the church's need to be both a prophetic voice and a haven for transformation and healing.

I realized that this dual career in service and silence had made deception a necessary survival tactic—lying not only to protect my identity but also creating a distance from genuine human connection. This chapter strives to untangle these threads, highlighting the tension between who I presented to the world and the true self I strived to embrace, hidden beneath layers of fear and tradition. In many ways, the church gave me purpose. It gave me community, stability, and structure. But it also gave me a place to prolong a conflicted life. It gave me a place to disappear—a role I could play without revealing the parts of my life that did not align with its teachings. That duality was both a gift and a burden.

CHAPTER 4

CRACKS BEGIN TO SHOW

As time wore on, my relationship with my wife had few conversations that vanished like smoke in the wind. What had once been a marriage full of shared dreams gradually turned into a partnership of logistics. It felt less like a bond of love and more like a mutual agreement focused on bills, schedules, and shared responsibilities. Somewhere along the way, love had slipped out of the fine print. In general, U.S. society began to change, and an ever-opening attitude towards gay issues continued. What is amazing to me is that we carried the same pattern of denial our parents had in life in our marriage. I never heard my parents discuss nor openly display anything that would be close to sexuality in their marriage. My wife never really discussed gay issues or popular media that featured gay couples and singers starting to come out. It felt like there was an unspoken presence in our marriage—a significant issue that loomed large yet remained unaddressed. It was the 'elephant in the room'—massive, obvious, and silently looming. We both saw it, but neither of us dared to name it. That's what every day felt like: walking around the truth too heavy to carry and too dangerous to speak directly about. During my years as a pastor, my role was to guide others and provide counseling through their own relationship challenges, referring many to professional help when needed. Ironically, while I served as a counselor to my congregation, offering sage advice and encouragement to seek professional guidance, I found it difficult to confront the struggles within my own marriage. My wife and I never considered seeking the same support I advised others to pursue, even as the unaddressed issues grew into a significant block in our relationship.

In recent years, sociologists have started naming a phenomenon that once went unspoken—marriages where emotional closeness remains, but physical intimacy fades. These are termed 'Dry Marriages.' While some see this as a red flag, our experience challenged that notion. While some viewed physical connection as essential, our relationship thrived on shared values and a commitment to supporting our LGBTQ+ friends and the broader community. Yet, the growing tension between my public persona and private reality intensified my internal conflict, ultimately pushing me to recognize the need for personal help. This journey taught me the importance of honesty and seeking guidance, no matter one's role or title in life. I think this irony wasn't due to ignorance, but perhaps a shared understanding—an unspoken agreement that growth and depth in our relationship didn't hinge solely on physicality. Instead, we found joy in the many dimensions of our companionship, leaving us to question society's definitions and find solace in the authentic connections we nurtured. But the reality was that we began to drift further apart, and our closeness faded as time went on. We began to drift apart as life demanded more from us. Parenting, careers, and the daily grind pulled us in different directions, leaving less space for connection. At the same time, my role as pastor was evolving, and with it, so was I. The shifts in our marriage mirrored a deeper transformation taking place within me—one that would soon spill into every corner of my life. Deep inside, I began to sense that my message and mission as a pastor were losing their vitality. Recognizing this stagnation sparked a realization: it was time for a change. This led me to entertain the possibility of a career shift, seeking fulfillment beyond the pulpit. Leaving the church felt like another full time job—emotionally, spiritually, and practically. Untangling myself from a community, a calling, and an identity I carried for decades wasn't something I could easily just walk away from. When we set our roots down in Spokane, I couldn't have foreseen that this would be the final congregation I'd shepherd as a pastor. The decision unfolded quietly, over years of reflection and inner growth. After two decades dedicated to spiritual leadership, this marked both the end and the exciting start of my professional journey, embarking on new opportunities and personal growth.

This realization marked both an ending and an exciting beginning—I submitted my resignation and went back to the university to obtain a master's degree in education to be a classroom teacher, bringing a host of valuable life experiences to the classroom. The job market was good, and immediately I took a job in a middle school teaching with a sense of accomplishment. Leaving the church was a relief, and the pressure was off me trying to speak about things I did not do in my own life. There were some Sundays I would stare at the congregants and think they have no idea what I am dealing with in my own life. I would call them to authenticity and being real with the God who loves them just the way they are. On the outside, we appeared to be a happily married couple—an image sustained by my belief that my wife was content. It was perhaps this very facade that kept us from acknowledging the unmet needs beneath it all, maintaining a veneer of normalcy that overlooked deeper issues.

The day we decided to sleep in separate bedrooms marked a significant turning point in our marriage. This quiet decision brought to light the unspoken truths that had long lingered between us. Reflecting on our journey, marrying seemed like a significant misstep, overshadowed by hidden desires I struggled to acknowledge. This decision signified not just physical distance but an acknowledgment of the emotional gulf that had grown, prompting deeper introspection about the path we had taken and the secrets quietly steering my life. I had clung to the hope that embracing heterosexual norms would somehow dissolve the yearnings that coursed beneath the surface of my soul— yearnings for a different kind of connection that never faded. As time passed, small fissures in our marriage inevitably became apparent. Yet, these cracks did not create enemies; rather, we maintained a façade of contentment, hand in hand in the eyes of the world. We lived under the illusion that maintaining external appearances equated to internal tranquility, avoiding the void that silently persisted between shared spaces and nightly rituals. Deep inside, we both navigated this silence, becoming co-conspirators in an unexamined life. Bound by a mutual reluctance to confront unspoken truths, our marriage was a facade of peace—an illusionary reality that shielded us from the depth of emotional connection we needed. This avoidance left us stranded in a space where true understanding and intimacy proved elusive, ultimately steering us on separate paths amidst a life unfulfilled.

CHAPTER 5

A SHATTERED SILENCE

As time lingered on, our conversations faded into sporadic whispers, vanishing like smoke in the wind. What started as a marriage began morphing into a mere partnership—more about managing finances and future investments than nurturing love. It seemed as if we had accidentally signed a pact that omitted love from the fine print, leaving us in a lonely silence. In this quietness, the atmosphere thickened, foretelling shifts yet to come. I couldn't ignore the growing void between us, accentuated by unspoken truths lingering like shadows. This silence, both profound and oppressive, hinted at the emotional chasms developing beneath the surface. As I continued down this path, introspection forced me to confront our journey and the secrets that had been steering my life unacknowledged. The time had come when we both grew weary of maintaining the facade of a marriage propped up with effort all this time. On the outside, we appeared to be a happily married couple—an image upheld by my belief that my wife was content. Perhaps it was this very facade that kept us from acknowledging the unmet needs beneath it all. The day we decided to sleep in separate bedrooms marked a significant turning point. This quiet decision highlighted the 50 unspoken truths long between us. As I reflect on our journey, marrying seemed like a misstep, overshadowed by hidden desires I struggled to acknowledge. This decision symbolized not just physical distance but an acknowledgment of the emotional gulf that had grown between us, prompting deeper introspection about the path we had taken and the secrets steering my life. Gradually, signs of our disconnect emerged, casting shadows that lengthened with each passing day. Our synchronized life rhythm faltered; meals became solitary rituals, with her overtime hours growing longer, leaving silence to fill the spaces once vibrant with shared laughter. Both adept at evasion, I was all too familiar with avoiding harsh truths. Now, witnessing her retreat into the same silence I knew well, the words we left unspoken were palpable. In our shared silence, a disconnection fermented that was anything but static—it felt akin to a ticking time bomb. Each unsaid word was another ominous step toward an inevitable detonation. This intensified separation bore the weight of unaddressed issues, threatening to expand into a chasm so wide that the hope of reconciliation felt as distant as a forgotten dream. Beneath the quiet lay a path fraught with tension, paved with unexpressed fears that neither of us dared to voice. Daily, the gap widened, with my awareness sharpening in the silent intervals, realizing that the void wasn't merely an absence of conversation—it was a growing specter of truth I needed to confront. Communication, the lifeline of any meaningful relationship, had frayed entirely, culminating in avoidance and a separation that spoke volumes in its silence. The realization hit that she seemed to have given up. Her exhaustion from the unending charade of our "marriage" had seeped into her every gesture and word. We had danced around our issues for so long that the complexity of our shared life now felt stripped down to a game—one not all parties wanted to play anymore, even in silence. As our family settled into Spokane, the backdrop of our lives seemed idyllic. We built our home in the suburbs, embraced my promising new job in the public school system, and enjoyed the perks of top-notch health insurance and individual cars. Our boys thrived in sports, drawing us into a whirlwind of practices and competitions. Outwardly, we maintained the appearance of a picture-perfect family, but beneath that veneer, our middle age crept in, shifting dreams and desires imperceptibly. The daily grind and growing responsibilities pushed aspects of our relationship, like intimacy, to the periphery—shadows of deeper changes unfolding. As we grew apart emotionally, I still clung to the façade of normalcy, intent on preserving the tranquility we displayed to the world. It was a quiet, poignant reflection of our combined resolve to maintain appearances, even as the distance between us expanded beyond words. In the solitude of those efforts, I found myself contemplating the delicate act of maintaining an outwardly harmonious existence among the shifting sands of internal truths. Silence crept into spaces once filled with laughter and connection. For us, avoidance has become not just a habit but a survival tactic. In my life, evasion had long been a coping mechanism, and now I saw her stepping into a similar darkness—a place where unspoken words became painfully clear. We didn't talk about the truth much because acknowledging it meant facing the possibility that everything could crumble between us. One crisp fall afternoon, I sat amidst the quiet solitude of our home. The silence was punctuated only by the faint rustling sounds from above as my wife moved about the house. Immersed in my schoolwork, I was startled when she called my name. Hearing her footsteps descending the stairs, a mix of anticipation and anxiety welled within me. This call made me nervous since we hadn't had a real conversation in weeks, and the air felt heavy with the weight of unspoken words. As she appeared at the top of the stairs, her expression was a blend of determination and courage. This unexpected approach, coupled with the looming silence between us, added tension to a moment that promised to be pivotal and perhaps revealing. "Can we talk?" she ventured, each syllable a tentative bridge reaching out across our dividing silence—a plea for connection amidst the echoes of estrangement. It was a question that hung in the air, heavy with the potential to fracture or to heal. The world seemed to pause for an instant when she delivered the question that would change everything: "How long have you known you are gay?" Her words landed with startling clarity and gravity. As the room seemed to spin around me, my heart pounded in my chest. She fixed her gaze on me, waiting for a response. My mind raced, frantically searching for an answer that would respect the seriousness of the moment and address the true depth of my reality. The silence stretched, heavy with anticipation and the weight of unspoken truths, leaving me to navigate a multitude of emotions. Her question sliced through the layers of carefully constructed deflections I'd erected over years, a direct challenge to confront the truth I'd kept buried. As my chest tightened, I fumbled for the right words. "I am not gay," I managed to say, my voice strained and fragile, as I clung to a facade I struggled to maintain. Misery laced my denial, contrasting sharply with the irony in the word "gay," which suggests happiness. As she turned to leave, I murmured, "I'm miserable, in fact, most of my life." This admission marked the beginning of unveiling my lifelong secret. We both agreed that it was time for me to move out, to find a place of my own where the boys could visit easily. This decision, intended to ease the transition for everyone, was heavy with sadness—a poignant acknowledgment of the fracture that had grown between us. As she left the room, all I could do was bury my face in weeping. There it was—an unintended confession, pulled into the open where it could no longer be ignored. Her bravery forced my hand, pulling the truth into light with an emotional gravity that felt both terrifying and liberating. Our shared silence was broken, and amidst the echoes of the past, a new conversation sparkled with the possibility of authenticity. Faced with the moment of raw truth that she unearthed, my life pivoted. It was her courage that gifted me the strength to break the silence that had been my constant companion. For those who identify with LGBTQ, I wish I could recount a heroic coming-out story, where valor propelled me into the open with pride. But the reality for me was quite different. The realization that I, myself, lacked the courage to step into my truth alone was daunting. It was her boldness that pushed open the door I had long feared, revealing both vulnerability and possibility beneath the light of acceptance. The journey was less a conquest and more a gradual emergence— where bravery lay not in loud proclamations, but in quiet acknowledgment and the soft, steady steps toward authenticity. Here I was in my 60s, and after more than 30 years of marriage, that night was the night my world, my life, would never be the same. In my head, this was the beginning of the end. I spent many sleepless nights trying to figure it out and what to do, and began to find an apartment close by with the thought the boys could visit and try to make this as normal as possible. The house was still, save for the muted sounds of my world unraveling. Late that night, as silence thickened the air, I listened to her sorrow seeping through the vent system—her weeping, an uncontrollable wail, reaching into the darkness with an almost unbearable poignancy. My heart clenched, caught between the instinct to comfort and the hesitation born of a widening chasm between us. That night stretched into shadows, a reminder of the turmoil we shared yet stood apart from. The following morning, she left for work, her absence marking a void that filled our home. As we were all getting ready for school, my sons approached me with innocent questions: "Dad, why was Mom so sad last night?" Their queries pierced me with a helplessness that stopped my voice short. In these times, I was at a loss for words; this situation had made its mark on the entire family. I wanted to tell them more of why 'Mom' was hurting but just couldn't find the words. "I don't know," I replied softly, masking the truth in uncertainty. "But you can give her hugs when you see her again tonight; I am sure she would appreciate that." A placating gesture, inadequate yet all I could manage in that trembling moment. Right then and there, I wanted to hug them both and tell them how sorry I was for hurting their mom. I fought back tears as we rode to school, ready to face another school day. As life ushered us forward, a fragile version of normalcy settled over us. Daily, I carried an unshakeable fear: not just of what had already been unraveled, but of what still waited in the silence, waiting to be spoken. I didn't know what healing would look like, or if I was even ready for it, but something had shifted. The silence had been broken. For the first time, I faced truths I had long avoided and hidden. The room filled with an uncomfortable truth, courageously revealed by her. I was caught between fear and relief, unsure of which emotion dominated. One thing was certain: our lives would never be the same. The silence had been broken. And for the first time, I was listening to the truth I had avoided and hidden for most of my life.

CHAPTER 6

BEGIN AGAIN

As I stood on the brink of separation, the reality of facing life without the structured foundation of marriage was overwhelming. Throughout my life, I had always been "taken care of"—first by my mother, and then by the stability of married life. Living alone for the first time brought a significant degree of anxiety. The prospect of doing so was daunting, as I navigated the solitude and the stress it brought, facing the unknown with a degree of uncertainty I had never experienced. It was as if I were about to embark on a journey without a map, compelled to navigate the complexities of a new existence where each decision felt fraught with tension and unpredictability. This transition marked the beginning of a daunting yet transformative chapter in my life. There was little emotional experience to lean on for success in this uncharted territory. How would I manage cooking or ensuring that finances stretched just enough for independence in my own apartment? Each practical consideration spun my thoughts into a whirlwind of anxiety.

Adding to this weighty uncertainty was the pressing question of communication— wondering who would inform the boys, our friends, or anyone who'd inevitably ask about my sudden absence from our shared life. It felt like stepping off a precipice into the unknown, with nothing but hope that I'd land on solid ground. Looking back on those pivotal moments, I now see that what felt like the end was, in reality, the dawn of a new beginning. Initially, the process of writing this memoir—reliving and confronting the layered complexities of my past—felt like navigating a maze filled with heavy echoes and unresolved truths. At the time, it seemed like life itself was unraveling. Yet, through this journey of reflection, I've come to realize how those endings paved the way for transformation and growth, where each challenge became the seed for renewal. This duality of experiencing both endings and new beginnings at once revealed the profound complexity and beauty of life's journey.

One thing that has enabled me to go on in life is the absolute hard-core rule of NOT living in the past. During this time of solitude, I began to spiral down into deep depression and remorse. I really didn't see how I was going to survive. As I continued to work as a teacher, it took up a good deal of time, allowing me to be with other people. I needed someone to talk to, and when my friend leaned in to listen intently, I felt a wave of relief. The need to confide in someone about my struggles was pressing, yet articulating the complexities without revealing my full truth was daunting. Lunch with a trusted colleague, who had been a pillar of support, seemed like a small step toward clarity. I shared the impending separation and looming divorce with a voice tinged with uncertainty. Her response—grounded in concern—breached the surface of my silence: "Get some professional help; you two can't give up on your marriage yet." Her words were both a call to action and a reflection of hope, stirring the unresolved tension within me—highlighting the pressing need for genuine support in a journey I hadn't fully embarked upon.

Finally, I said the words I thought I would never hear come from my mouth: "I THINK I AM GAY!" The words felt sharp in my mouth, foreign and even raw, but these simple words shattered the lies and silence I had been hiding all my life. Saying those words was so uncomfortable, "I think I am gay." At least I had verbalized the recent events to some other human beings, and I felt less isolated and alone.

Amidst the unraveling of my marriage, the pressing need to stay connected with my two sons became paramount. The priority of sitting down with them was shadowed by an aching vulnerability, an intense longing for emotional contact tempered by the fear of what such a conversation might reveal. The thought of sharing this new reality filled me with apprehension, as I navigated the complexity of maintaining a bond amidst shifting family dynamics. This conversation was a pivotal moment, one that would change the landscape of our family dynamics forever. We gathered for lunch, the usual comfort now overshadowed by the weight of my revelation. My heart pounded in my chest as I began to speak, each word laden with fear and a careful hope for understanding. I explained to them that their mother and I would be separating, leading eventually to a divorce, and the truth I had kept hidden for so long—I believed I was gay.

The response was silence; they continued to eat, eyes fixed on their plates, an impenetrable wall of indifference or perhaps shock. "Do you have any questions for me?" I asked, my voice betraying the tremors of my heart. My eldest son finally spoke, "So, let me get this right—you gave up staying withMom and our family for having sex with men?" His words hit with a sharpness I hadn't expected. His words stung! As they rose and left, their retreat echoed loudly in my heart. Left alone at the table, tears streamed down my face, each one a testament to the fear of losing their love and the desperation of seeking my own truth.

As I sat at the table, I realized that my sons might need some distance to process the looming divorce. The thought of how they would perceive a father who is gay was daunting. I hoped desperately that we would remain close; I feared losing them from my life. In that moment, I found myself exposed—a father yearning for acceptance, yet aware of the complex journey we were all about to start. Sitting alone in my sparsely furnished apartment, I felt the weight of my new reality pressing down on me. Reality had struck hard and fast, revealing that despite being close enough to see my former home from my window, the emotional distance was far greater than I anticipated. My sons didn't visit or reach out, leaving me with an overpowering sense of invisibility and isolation. As I sat on the old wooden apple crate that served as my makeshift chair, I couldn't ignore the profound sense of solitude.

As some of these first revelations came about and some truths emerged, the path forward was fraught with challenges. I was afraid to live in the truth. It was so much more comfortable hiding in the secret I had kept most of my life. The realization dawned heavily around me: embracing change wouldn't shield me from the storms to come, but it marked the beginning of a journey where I had to find resilience amidst uncertainty.

CHAPTER 7

EMBRACING SOLITUDE—
REALLY?

Standing amidst the bare walls of my new apartment, an unfamiliar solitude wrapped around me like a shroud. The scent of fresh paint lingered, marking a stark contrast to the warmth of my former home. Each room was empty, echoing with possibilities yet unfilled by life. I knew this space wasn't just a temporary stop; it would become my home, as the reality of my separation loomed larger. No longer could I view this place as a mere layover, like a hotel, before returning to my past life—I had to embrace the challenge of forging a new beginning here, one room at a time, as I slowly transformed this empty apartment into a reflection of my new reality. Every room held both a challenge and an opportunity, inviting me to introspection as I navigated the uncharted waters of single life. Adjusting to independence involves grappling with fear—the fear of isolation, of self-sufficiency, and the unknown future. I had no roadmap from my childhood for living independently, and after almost 50 years of being interdependent, the idea of standing on my own felt frightening. I had to learn daily basic skills and try to replace my fears with personal strength and resilience. My family life was a bustling home filled with activity; now my reality stood in sharp contrast to my isolation, illustrating how much I yearned for that continual energy and connection. Despite working full-time at a challenging middle school, I sought out part-time jobs during the evenings, grasping for distractions that kept solitude at bay. The thought of facing my apartment's silence was daunting, amplifying the loneliness that crept in through its walls. Navigating this maze of uncertainty and newfound independence, I questioned the strength of friendships that once seemed unwavering, now obscured by shifting life circumstances. Each day blurred into the next, driven by a desperate need to anchor myself in activity as I grappled with the hard reality of standing on my own. Sometimes just running into church members while shopping, their well-meaning words often filled me with a deep sting. "We're all praying for you," they would say, and earnestly add, "praying you don't pursue that homosexual lifestyle." Each encounter was a poignant reminder of the rumors swirling around me, wrapped in spiritual good intentions but laden with judgment. These interactions cut deeply, highlighting the painful juxtaposition of support and the underlying assumptions about my life, leaving me with a lasting ache in their wake. Securing a part-time job selling shoes at Nordstrom, driven partly by the potential for a generous commission, provided both a financial lifeline and an essential distraction. The allure of work extended beyond necessity—it was also an escape, a place where silence didn't stalk my every move. Tackling a full-time teaching role at a challenging middle school and supplementing it with evening and weekend work left me exhausted. The relentless grind made me question my effectiveness and engagement with my middle school students. Yet, amid the fatigue, the true struggle lay in the gradual realization that my journey required a significant courage I was building day by day. Navigating the ambiguity of friendships also weighed heavily, as the lines blurred between genuine connection and the polite camaraderie of colleagues. It's all about letting go of my preconceived notions of what life should be and instead embracing what it is not. By confronting solitude, I can redefine my identity outside the context of relationships or societal expectations. Each day, I hoped my two sons would call or text, wanting to check in. Every buzz of my phone brought hope. But it was never them. The silence stung in ways I didn't know were possible. In Spokane, there was a robust sports program that meant both my sons were constantly busy—

from nightly practices to weekends filled with games. Their time was so consumed, it was easy to understand why they didn't reach out. Given all that was happening, I could see why they might struggle to find the words or the time to ask how I was doing, but it hurt.For me, being alone isn't merely about physical solitude; it represents a passage towards understanding oneself better, embracing one's imperfections, and ultimately finding peace and direction in life. There were many nights I found myself grappling with the silence, either weeping into the depths of my pillow until exhaustion took over, or staring at the glowing digits of my alarm clock as they crept toward the early hours, keeping company with my restless thoughts. It was during these moments of solitude and introspection that I realized the profound need for professional help. Confronting my fears and insecurities felt both overwhelming and essential. Each day seemed both fleeting and endless, wrapped in uncertainty and the longing for clarity. Eventually, I gathered the courage to begin to reach out, understanding that I needed someone to listen—to guide me through the transformative phase of my life. The nights were heavy with quiet and self-reflection, a solitude that became a profound journey of introspection and self-discovery. It was during these hours of silence that I began to rebuild my identity, confronting fears and examining the life I'd led. Writing this memoir forces me to delve deep into my past—exploring intense and defining moments that shaped my being. It's a process that slowly fosters clarity and a deeper understanding of who I am. This is not just about learning to be content alone; it's about embracing life independently and authentically. Though the journey started with trepidation, it evolved into a powerful path toward self-acceptance. In my darkest moments, ending it all seemed like the easiest route—but something, I still don't know what, kept me tethered to life. I understood then that I wanted to live, to find a new life of happiness if that was possible. Seeking professional help became a crucial turning point. It wasn't easy, but it was essential—a decision that affirmed my commitment to life and the pursuit of joy beyond the pain. My journey with therapy introduced me to varied experiences with professionals. It quickly became evident that many therapists concluded our sessions with another round of prescriptions, proposing they would help me sleep, calm down, and find my way back to "normal." This isn't a criticism of psychology as a profession, but an observation of the generalized approach adopted by some practitioners. At a time when I craved insightful understanding and a reliable ear, these interactions often left me feeling unheard and unclear about the path to healing. After many visits with therapists, I found an older female therapist who didn't begin with what about medication aids. She listened for an hour and just asked if she could help me. I teared up at her kind offer. From that moment, we worked together, and it took hours for me to pour over my history and background with little or no comments on her part. I felt relief and a small sense of calm and actually looked forward to coming to her small, unkempt office each week. She didn't address the five different meds I was taking from the host of other professionals who prescribed these essential aids to my healing; she seemed not to care. When I asked her, she said that was my choice. I wasn't quite sure about the word "choice" at this stage in my life. In 1975, I graduated from college and seminary in Philadelphia. However, moving from the East to the West Coast for ministry led me to lose touch with many colleagues. Suddenly, a phone call in the middle of the night changed everything. It was Jeff from Maine, now Dr. Leonards, a brilliant student and close friend from my past. After writing several books, Dr. Jeff had a successful psychiatry practice. I was surprised and relieved to hear his voice; I poured out my heart, confessing my feelings of despair and the troubling thought of ending my life. Jeff, understanding and direct, reminded me of the legacy I could leave for my sons, urging me to find reasons to live. His candid yet gentle words were a lifeline. When I mentioned my heavy reliance on various medications, his concern was palpable. He insisted I wean off the addictive pills cautiously, starting with specific guidance. As the call ended, his final words—"Ken, you are loved! Don't forget it"—echoed in my heart. This connection revitalized my Spirit, sparking a gradual journey toward healing and acceptance. I don't know about you, but the higher power, God, or whatever spiritual force moved the circumstances for this amazing phone call. I have spoken to Dr. Jeff many more times, with his goal to make sure I weaned off the drugs and began to take control of my own life on my own power, which I thought was impossible before that call. I connected with another human being far from me on the East Coast. I had so much to share with my therapist. The next week I told her the whole story, and she just smiled and said she was proud of me. While the weekly therapy was crucial to bringing some emotional healing, my spiritual world remained in flux. I had the deep desire to attend church. Most of the time, I would slip into the back rows of the various churches I would visit for fear someone would recognize me from my church work. The intent to maintain my connection to faith was there, but I found myself feeling like an outcast in a setting that should have offered sanctuary. As different preachers spoke, reflecting on love yet often condemning same-sex relationships, a rift appeared in my acceptance of their words. I couldn't help but dissect the sermons, often thinking, "I don't believe that anymore." Each Sunday sent me on a journey through big and small churches alike, those deemed safely conservative evangelical. I was searching for a place where my evolving views and sense of self could harmonize with teachings from the pulpit, yet each visit seemed to deepen the chasm between what I once believed and what my heart now understood. The experience was isolating but also enlightening, carving a path toward authenticity and acceptance in the midst of spiritual transformation. During a particularly challenging phase, I entered a medium-sized Lutheran church. At first, the unfamiliar environment— candles, robes, and formal liturgy— was uncomfortable. But the messages centered on grace and love, offering what I hadn't realized I was seeking. An encounter with the assistant pastor led to a candid conversation over coffee about my life's upheaval, and he encouraged me to come back. Gradually, I found a place in the community, drawn to the teachings despite my emotional numbness. Every Sunday, the act of participating in communion emerged as a pivotal moment. As I moved forward with the congregation to receive the sacred elements, each kneel at the altar felt transformative, offering a profound sense of connection and humility. This ritual, transcending the ordinary, anchored me amid life's uncertainties, grounding me with fragments of peace and meaning that spurred my spiritual healing.

CHAPTER 8

THE PATHWAY OF THERAPY AND UNLEARNING

One weekend, feeling lost within myself, I wandered into a quiet bookstore and stumbled across "A Life of Unlearning" by Australian Pastor Anthony Venn-Brown. I wasn't looking for hope, but somehow, I found it in those pages. It became a book that I devoured in half a day. This book profoundly reshaped my journey of self-discovery. His story mirrored my own narrative: a married preacher struggling with his sexuality. Each narrative echoed my struggles and uncertainties, offering a reflective mirror. These insights challenged the frameworks I'd known, guiding me toward a life anchored in authenticity. It felt serendipitous, as if every word had been crafted with my path in mind, leading me through the labyrinth of faith, identity, and growth. This wonderful book became the bridge to the beginning of a new chapter—a pathway of therapy and unlearning, where I could finally start to understand and accept myself.

I had high hopes that I would find a person offering new insights and that the whole experience would be transformative as I healed. I went to four different therapists, all with impressive credentials. I learned quickly that too many therapists seemed to reach for their prescription pads while listening to my story. I wasn't looking for medication; I was searching for meaning, for someone who could help me rewrite the story of my life. I wanted to redefine my identity. I wanted to learn to navigate new life circumstances with support and guidance and maybe find a path back to my family. Deep down, I wanted my life back, and with more meaning than before. I wanted healing, but on my terms, and certainly not with four different psychotropic drugs to enable me to function.

I think therapy is supposed to help individuals address mental illness and empower them to understand and reshape life's narrative, which would, I think, lead to a more fulfilling and authentic life. I continued my search for that one special person who would listen. Some sessions lasted briefly as they took out their prescription pads to write a new drug to help and do away with the last prescription the previous professional had written. If you are a professional therapist and are offended by my words, I ask you to think about the number of prescriptions you write while you are supposed to be listening to the client. In my search for help, the professionals I encountered seemed to expect I'd simply schedule another session, yet many lacked a concrete plan or a clear direction for our journey together. I realized that what I truly sought was guidance—a roadmap to navigate the therapy process and find clarity in the chaos of my emotions. This experience taught me that while therapy can be impactful, not every encounter will fit the needs of each individual's unique journey. It was a pivotal realization in understanding what I needed from therapy and what my path to healing would require.

So you can see how these appointments were going. All this time, I was still working two jobs: 8:00 AM to 4:30 PM at school and 5:00 PM to 11:00 PM selling shoes. For me, this was the only way to ensure I stayed busy and did not entertain thoughts of being alone and falling into a deeper depression. Therapy, at its best, invites us to think differently about our reality. My therapist didn't hand me answers, but her questions challenged me to dig deeper. And that made all the difference. Finding someone besides yourself and friends who can give you a different perspective is invaluable. For me, it was worth the time and discipline. When you encounter the "right" person, an indescribable, almost sacred resonance fills the air—a moment where words and understanding align perfectly. As she gently sipped her tea, her nod acknowledged the profound connection we shared during our conversations. It felt like those sessions were more than just appointments; they were lifelines extended across time and space, a deliberate weaving of shared experiences and reflections.

During one session, she paused, looked at me, and asked a pointed question that unlocked a door in my thinking, a door I hadn't dared open. When I left her office that afternoon, I knew I had found someone who saw me. The exchange I experienced in therapy was transformative, transcending the traditional boundaries of a typical session. It became evident that she truly valued our time, ensuring future meetings were always planned. Each nod and sip of tea symbolized a growing trust and understanding between us. This connection was not just about addressing present concerns but about untangling the past—a journey of unlearning. I realized the need for new thinking and actions, and most importantly, a commitment to start telling the truth. It was clear that I had much to "unlearn," setting the stage for a more authentic way of living.

CHAPTER 9

❖━━━━━━━━❖

GRIEF, LOVE, AND LETTING GO!

Spokane, a mid-sized town rich with memory and familiarity, was also home to my elderly mother. She lived in a retirement center, surrounded by friends and conversation, finding joy in daily routines and closeness to family. To her, it was a peaceful life. But I was about to shatter that peace with a truth she wasn't ready for. Determined to embrace authenticity, I faced the challenge of truth-telling, particularly with my mother. As I sat across from her, the weight of what needed to be said hung heavily between us. When I revealed my separation and solitude, her familiar face was etched with the wisdom of years—and it crumbled into tears. It wasn't just the news of my life changes that stung; it was a break from the dreams she held for her "favorite son." This moment was an emotional turning point, underscoring the deep impact of honesty on our connection. I shared with her that my marriage was over. In her traditional Baptist fashion, she reacted with hopeful defiance— "You don't give up. My kids don't give up. I taught you better with faith." Her voice, though trembling, carried years of faith and expectation. She insisted that through prayer, there would be resolution, even as I grappled with the haunting finality of my words. This moment of raw, emotional tension— forged in love and misunderstandings spoke volumes about the generational gap in understanding and the deep-seated bonds of family ties.

As time went on, my mother remained steadfast in her determination to see our family reconciled. Each conversation with her was an exercise in optimism, and I found myself wanting to share positive updates. "I'm seeing a good spiritual counselor," I told her, reassuring her of my regular church attendance. One day, she expressed her intention to call my wife, hopefully to bridge the gap. I gently reminded her that giving my wife space and time to process everything was essential. "Let's just keep praying for her and the boys," I suggested, aiming to keep things simple yet heartfelt—a reminder that though things were complex, they were handled with care and love. I just couldn't bring myself to tell her the real reason my marriage had ended. All my life, I wanted to shield her from this truth, believing it would hurt her more than heal. So, instead, I became her personal errand boy, filling in the spaces where conversation avoided what neither of us dared say. I didn't tell her about the medications or about taking another job to stay busy. She relied upon me for everything, and now it was no excuse to be with me. "I need sugar. I need some toilet paper." There were no lists on purpose. During a visit to my mother's apartment, she revealed she had spoken with a local pastor who specialized in marriage counseling. To my surprise, she had already arranged for him to visit and help mend my broken marriage. Her well-intentioned intervention ignited a strong emotional response in me—part anger, part desperation. Though her actions were driven by love and hope, the unexpected confrontation with this pastor forced me to confront the intensity of my feelings. It was a pivotal moment that underscored the complexity of our relationship, as I grappled with both the depth of her care and the boundaries I needed to establish.

I held her hand and said she didn't understand the whole story and pleaded with her to STOP. I tried to be as spiritual as I could by telling her, "Promise me, we will let God work and move; the best thing she could do for me and my marriage was to pray and stay out of it. PLEASE!" A few months went on in which our time together was filled with discussion of marriage, scripture verses, and prayer cards she would make for me to display in my car and in my apartment. By this point, it seemed the entire retirement center, plus the staff, was praying for me. My name had made it onto prayer chains, bulletin boards, and coffee hour conversations. I could only smile at the irony and divine intervention by committee. As the days unfolded, my mother's hope and faith remained steadfast; she was convinced that God would guide us back together in time. Yet, shadowed by her optimism was a restlessness—she confided in me that she wasn't sleeping well, her thoughts consumed by worry. My mother's life became increasingly uncomfortable while living with my brother due to his struggles with alcoholism. Despite missing Michigan, she faced a difficult decision—unable to live independently, yet wary of returning to a precarious situation. The weight of this choice, steeped in the complexities of family loyalty and personal well-being, added layers of tension and concern to an already challenging situation. The very notion sent a chill through my veins—a foreboding feeling that enveloped my heart. It was the fear of what might lie ahead, the uncertainty of an unknown future, and the quiet desperation of feeling helpless to prevent a path that seemed destined to unfold. This was more than just a consideration; it was a crossroads bathed in the shadows of what family decisions often entail—choices that ripple through time, altering the lives they touch.

Now there was an additional worry for me: my mother. I loved her so much, and it depressed me more to witness her strength fade over this situation. In the middle of the night, I received a phone call from the retirement center saying my mother had fallen out of bed and was on her way to the hospital. I panicked at the thought of a 91-year-old woman with broken bones. I got dressed and rushed to the emergency room, where she was lying in pain with an attending doctor. The doctor told me she had fractured her hip and needed surgery immediately. I felt so alone, but I had to call my brother in Michigan. He said little and hung up. Gratefully and surprisingly, she went through the surgery just fine, and in two days was released to a rehabilitation center to gain strength.

My therapy and worry about myself were put on hold as I visited her daily. It took her just a few days, and she was ready to continue the charge to find a solution to my situation. I couldn't hold it in any longer. "Mom, please stop! My marriage isn't going to be fixed. I am homosexual." Her response was like a splash of cold water: "When did this start? Why don't you go see a doctor and get this fixed?" Her words, filled with misunderstanding, were a harsh reminder of our differing perspectives. Despite my frustration, I recognized her reaction came from a place of concern and generational beliefs. Trying to navigate this response, while painful, was part of my journey toward self-acceptance. I was sick to my stomach as she looked away. I told her there were no solutions, no prayers, no fixes, and no Remedies. I told her briefly that I have struggled all my life. I told her I am sure my wife has been unhappy for most of our married life. Deep down, I thought I would never tell her, and probably until this day, I regret it. As I drove home, I stopped at a park because my eyes were filled with tears and I couldn't see to drive. I had to let her process this revelation, but at her age and in her life, that was nearly impossible. The conversation with my mother began again with a torrent of questions, each one laced with the desperation of a loving parent trying to understand a situation that defied her expectations. Faced with the reality I had long grappled with, I replied, "I think I was born this way. Maybe you gave birth to a gay son." Uttering those words felt like piercing through my own heart as I watched them land with a visible weight on her. I saw the hurt flicker across her face, a silent testament to the difficult realization we both now faced. Tears threatened to surface, and my resolve wavered as I suggested gently, "Maybe we can stop talking about this." Despite the sadness that lingered between us, a glimmer of solace emerged in her physical recovery. The joy of seeing her walk with a cane, strengthened through diligent therapy, became a beacon of hope that even in pain, healing was possible.

As I sat with my mother, a heartbreaking realization settled in—I was watching her transform before my very eyes. It felt as if the relentless passage of time had suddenly quickened, etching years into her gentle face with every word exchanged about my life's recent changes. The gravity of our conversation seemed to weigh relentlessly upon her, and my heart ached with the knowledge that my truths had unwittingly caused her pain and stress, hastening the signs of aging that I could see before my eyes. Seeing my once-strong mother appear fragile and worn before me was a deeply saddening moment, filled with a foreboding sense of helplessness and a yearning to protect her from the harsh realities I could no longer shield her from. The emotional depth of this realization left me feeling profoundly connected yet powerless, as if I, too, was swept along in the current of life's inexorable changes.

When I arrived at my mother's rehab room, she informed me of her decision to move back to Michigan with my brother. It felt like a blow to my very core— a gut-wrenching realization

that her pain was physically manifesting in her need to leave. She couldn't bear to remain, feeling helpless in the face of my hurt. The idea that leaving was her best way to cope left me stricken with sadness. Days went on, and her hip healed fine, but her heart was broken by her own son. I purchased two plane tickets, determined to escort her home, and on the flight, our hands remained linked—a tactile symbol of our deep bond—as she tenderly leaned her head on my shoulder. It was a journey filled with unspoken emotion, a shared understanding that this moment was a delicate balance of heartbreak and resolve.

As we arrived in Michigan, my brother was waiting in a parking lot. He didn't greet me. The sight of him taking her four packed suitcases and driving away marked the end of an era that I would never forget in my mind and would hold dear. In a few short months, my mother's life came to an abrupt end due to a massive stroke, leaving behind a silence so profound it could never be filled. The finality of her passing weighs heavily on my heart, haunted by the irreversible reality and plagued by doubts about whether my decisions were right. The ache of knowing I would never again hear her voice or feel her reassuring presence is a grief that lingers deeply, casting shadows over each moment of reflection. Her absence resonates with the undeniable finality of loss, underscoring the fragile nature of the time we share with those we love and the enduring impact their departure leaves in its wake. Yet deep within, I hold onto the truth that my mother loved me, even her 'gay son,' in a world that felt too much to bear at times for her.

I hope and pray she found peace in her sleep, leaving behind burdens and entering a comforting embrace beyond our world. There was an urgency for me to return to therapy; I wrestled with the profound task of integrating grief and seeking closure into my journey. The realization hit me hard that I never truly expressed to my mother how deeply I...loved her—how she was the best mother anyone could have had. Her passing forced childhood memories into sharp focus, creating an urgent need to find understanding and peace.

With both of my parents now gone and my older brother's sudden death a year later, I faced the somber reality of being the last remaining member of my family. This weight pressed heavily upon me, fueling a determination to seek healing and embrace the lessons of love and loss with courage and resolution. I don't think I resolved the grief to this day, but it did offer a sense of moving forward. It sparked new growth and a new understanding that prepares me for what comes next in my life. It seemed like my life was full of pain, but minus half of the psycho meds I was taking, I was finally able to live raw.

Everyone around me knew I was in deep pain, and few tried to offer words to touch my heart. Even my school principal took me aside and asked if I needed some time off. I was determined now to read and take in the gay world. I read every book I could get my hands on, even if I didn't understand half the content. I saturated myself with theology books, novels, and even gay romance books to fill my mind. As the culture gradually changed, there were many in and out of the institutional church writing with LGBTQ themes. This chapter of my life story is entitled "The Pain of Loss." I find myself reflecting on dual forms of profound realization. With the passing of my family members, I not only lost most of my blood relatives in this world but also acknowledged the culmination of an internal battle— for years, I had waged war against my own sexuality.

It was a writing on the wall, a truth long whispered only to myself, now echoing louder in the silence left by their absences. No longer would I dispute the profound realization that I was born gay; instead, I faced forward, committed to finding the strength to embrace this new reality. Through therapy, my sessions began to chart a path reflective of this profound acceptance, as I sought to reconcile my past with a newfound determination to journey forward authentically. The end of one chapter marked the beginning of another—a step into embracing. the breadth of who I am with courage and an open heart. The Pastor of the church I attended became a close mentor friend. The Lutheran Pastor friend once told me, "'Don't look back with regrets but look forward with hope," as he quoted the apostle Paul's admonition. When he told me this, I wasn't ready to hear these words. Now, at this time in my life, I have begun to 'UNLEARN' to look forward with HOPE! Using Anthony Venn Brown's words, my biggest task was now too much of what brought comfort, and yet I needed to ask why I was so comfortable with my past. I was determined to seek new insights and explore new thinking. I am also realizing that I am losing my own family and trying to reshape a new relationship with my sons. I don't get the opportunity to sit down and talk and understand each other. I know I caused each of them a degree of embarrassment and pain in their early growing years.

Since the divorce, my connection with my sons has become tenuous at best. Raised in a church atmosphere, they are still entrenched in those beliefs, grappling with discomfort regarding my being gay. Perhaps they carry a sense of shame, something unspoken yet deeply felt, creating a barrier between us. This distance pains me, a reminder of the close relationship we once had that now feels out of reach. Most of my close friends have advised me to give space and time to the relationships I hold dear with my sons. I hold tightly to the hope that they are right. I also sense that their emotional support leans heavily toward their mother, and understandably so, as she navigates her own journey through this change. While I harbor the hope that time will foster healing, I acknowledge that my wife may not share a positive reflection on the past we lived together. The unfolding of this reality is like interpreting a delicate dance of familial dynamics—a balance between giving love time to heal.

CHAPTER 10

A DAWN OF NEW REALITY

Deconstructing old beliefs has become a crucial part of my journey. It involves embracing new perspectives and beliefs, allowing me to align more closely with my true self. I didn't initially realize how essential this process was, particularly as my former theological views no longer served my current life's path. Honestly, I feared losing a part of my traditional beliefs, but I now understand the importance of unlearning and embracing my authentic self. As I began to unlearn my ingrained beliefs, I recognized that many did not align with my true identity. This journey involved confronting deeply accepted "truths" and was fraught with struggle. I had to ask myself: What was I willing to let go of, and where was I heading? Facing these uncomfortable truths became crucial if I wanted to find peace. It meant releasing the past and preconceived self-images to embrace serenity and authenticity. This is where I would turn to do some very eye-opening work in theology and philosophy. I had studied for three long years at seminary to learn about ancient scriptures. Never did the professors delve into homosexuality. I was quite aware of the numerous passages in the Bible that condemn same-sex attractions. I was also aware of the church and the condemnations of those who tried to legitimize their behavior. I reached out to seminary professors asking about any updates in theology, but received no response. I sought out some local churches that were open to the LGBTQ community, but there were few. At this time, there seemed to be a flood of written material in which I immersed myself. I started to see my time taken up reading, and I began to journal, which is the basis of this memoir. It wasn't a comfortable fit for me to sit and write, but then I filled pages with everything from my background to my new theological thoughts. Engaging with a variety of theological perspectives and interpretations provided a deeper understanding of this complex issue for me. Passages such as Leviticus 18:22 and Romans 1:26-27 are often cited in discussions about homosexuality. I noticed some of my liberal-minded friends would either ignore biblical passages that made them uncomfortable, much like conservatives ignore social justice passages of scripture. I came to the realization that ALL religious people pick and choose their 'holy grail'. For instance, I read that some scholars debate whether these passages condemn the act itself or specific practices of the time. What grounded me most throughout this whole theological journey was that my faith was always Christocentric. That is, it centered on the purpose, mission, and message of the historical person of Jesus Christ. I kept being drawn back to His words—His message resonated deeply with me. 91 But in hindsight, I realize that my Christocentric focus wasn't balanced by a broader, theocentric perspective—one that considers God the Father at the center. My theology leaned heavily toward Jesus without a fuller view of the Triune nature of God. Jesus was the fulfillment of the strict unbending law of God. Many believe the overarching message of Christianity is love, acceptance, and compassion for all individuals. I was satisfied that the teachings of Jesus were about loving one's neighbor and non-judgment. I also gained more insight that Jesus was a friend to the outcast. However, as I began delving into the historical and cultural contexts in which the Bible was written, a transformative clarity emerged. It was enlightening to see how these factors profoundly influence contemporary interpretations of scripture. This revelation brought an unexpected freedom to my life. I pondered whether I had learned this in seminary and somehow overlooked or ignored it entirely. Regardless, it was astonishing that I had preached and ministered for so many years without this understanding. For the first time, I embraced the truth that I am both gay and Christian, ready to live fully in this new, harmonized reality, where my faith and a new identity 92 found peace together. The more I took an honest examination of my faith, the less sense some of the core doctrines made, like my rigid ideas of heaven and hell or the overemphasis I put on a 'personal relationship with Jesus.' I started to see these as less absolute, and that shift brought unexpected freedom in my thinking. Facing the need to unlearn ingrained beliefs was daunting. My faith, shaped by years in the church, had masked an underlying intolerance toward others I hadn't fully recognized. Letting go of these outdated views was unsettling because I had accepted them as truths. Growing up, my journey was one of consistently finding myself out of step with my peers and even my family—a profound testament to the resilience and power of self-definition. From an early age, staying true to who I am meant challenging norms, not out of rebellion, but out of necessity. In a world often filled with predefined roles and expectations, I learned to stand firm, embodying my individuality. Whether it was choosing clothes that differed from those of my peers or passionately pursuing hobbies deemed unconventional, each decision became a bold declaration of self, etched into my story of growth and defiance against the tides of conformity. 93 As I matured, embracing a counter-culture identity became not merely a personal journey but a social statement, particularly poignant in the realm of my own gay reality. For those who identify within these spaces, every day represents a choice between conformity and authenticity. It's about carving out a presence in a world that sometimes still struggles to accept a broad spectrum of identities. I have avoided writing about gay culture and the enormous changes and acceptance occurring in American culture at the time, but the LGBTQ+ movement has rewritten narratives around what it means to exist authentically, providing a vital counterpoint to mainstream culture. Even an American president would come to embrace the change, which led the Supreme Court to declare same-sex marriage a legal right. That boy, now a man, has learned the power of community that comes with identifying proudly and supporting others in their journey. Attending my first Gay Parade in our small town was a moment of both nerves and revelation. As I stepped into the vibrant scene, I was surprised to encounter familiar faces—individuals I considered allies of the gay community. This event, filled with colors and solidarity, became a tapestry of shared joy and acceptance. It was a profound experience, one that highlighted the power of community and the comfort found in unity, lifting the veil of isolation I had felt for so long. In that moment, I wasn't just an observer; I was part of a collective voice celebrating authenticity and love. It struck me 94 how far I had come—from hiding, from shame, from isolation. Here, no one needed to be explained or justified. I was seen. I was safe, and for the first time in my life, I felt proud not just of who I was, but of how far I had come in my journey. In this evolving landscape, being part of a counter-culture extends beyond personal identity—it becomes a larger cultural dialogue. For many in the LGBTQ+ community, it's about impacting positive change and expanding societal understanding. Whether through activism, art, or simply living openly, these acts challenge others to rethink their perceptions. Each story shared, each coming out, is a step toward reshaping the broader narrative to be more inclusive and accepting. Through these life experiences, what once was merely counter becomes a powerful cultural shift, aligning personal truth with societal change. For me, it's not just about being different; it's about creating a world where diversity in identity and thought is celebrated as the norm. With time, I found myself less patient with anti-gay rhetoric. Where I once tried to reason or retreat, I knew I would push back. My tolerance for intolerance wore thin—but I also had to check myself. I wanted to fight ignorance without becoming bitter. How could I shout 'LOVE IS LOVE' and be unloving to those who didn't agree with me? 95 Amidst the emotional upheaval, I craved connection. Like many singles, I turned to the internet not to escape but to seek a lifeline. I soon found myself chatting with a gay English teacher in Brazil. Our conversations were initially a way for him to practice English, but they quickly became something I eagerly anticipated. Despite cultural differences that sometimes clouded our understanding, I cherished our heartfelt exchanges. Video chats added a layer of intimacy, making this unexpected friendship feel even more special and crucial during a time of great personal change. After the divorce, I faced the daunting task of navigating the holidays— those times formerly filled with the warmth of family, now marked by their absence. The notion of missing the shared meals at Thanksgiving and the joy of exchanging gifts at Christmas left me with a profound sense of loss. While grappling with this emptiness, I decided to leave my job at Nordstrom in large part supported by the encouragement of new friends who lifted my spirits. One friend, in particular, suggested an exciting escape: visiting an online friend in Brazil for the holidays. Though the thought was daunting, it stirred a flicker of excitement and possibility within me. Why not embrace the opportunity? So on Christmas Eve, with a daring spirit and a suitcase in hand, I set out on a journey that would ultimately change my life. Flying twelve hours from 96 Spokane to São Paulo, Brazil, on Christmas Day was an interesting reality for me. That trip was supposed to be a distraction, but it became a doorway. What started as online chats blossomed into a love story. My Brazilian friend became my husband, and Brazil became my new home—not just geographically, but emotionally and spiritually. Significantly, it was the first time I felt fully accepted and truly myself.

CHAPTER 11

DISCOVERING LOVE

As time went on, my connection with my Brazilian friend began to blossom into a deeper, cherished relationship. His support was unwavering—offering me a safe place to feel seen, affirmed, and loved. What started as an online connection became a source of hope, reminding me that living authentically and rediscovering love was not only possible but real and could genuinely flourish. I had to acknowledge that, despite our deepening connection, my Brazilian friend came from a different culture and background, each with its own personal challenges. Yet, he consistently offered me unwavering support and loving understanding. This mutual acceptance and empathy became the foundation upon which our relationship grew, enabling us to embrace one another's journeys with compassion and support.

I returned to my trusted therapist and started exploring the possibility of finding love again. What I mistook for apprehensions were actually three key insights about my personal life.

Therapist Insight on Self-Worth: She quickly pointed out a deep-seated character flaw: my belief that I might not deserve a fresh start. My entire life had been marked by putting my needs aside. She helped me confront my poor self-image, raising the question: Am I ready to be in a relationship? Poor self-image haunts my whole life.

Internal Conflict About Love and Sex: I learned that in the gay community, while many desire deep relationships, casual sex is often accepted. This clashed with my comfort level, as I couldn't imagine being intimate outside a committed relationship. More importantly, I questioned whether I was simply looking for a quick replacement to avoid being alone.

Readiness and Desire for Companionship: Over time, I've discovered that love is a process—it takes time to grow. Rediscovering love has been transformative. I now understand its depth and complexity, realizing that nurturing love requires vulnerability and patience. It's not about filling a void but about embracing genuine companionship and letting it flourish. Rediscovering love has been a transformative journey for me. In the past, I had known marital love, or at least what I thought love was supposed to be. Yet, it was only after facing deep personal valleys that I began to understand its true depth and complexity. The most unexpected part of this journey was how love, when tenderly nurtured, can grow into something far-reaching and profound. Initially, it was akin to stumbling upon a forgotten garden in my heart, where seeds of love had lain dormant for years, waiting silently for the right conditions to flourish.

Over time, I realized that nurturing love requires vulnerability and patience. I became more aware of love's subtleties, seeing it not in grand gestures but in simple, everyday

Kindness. Each act of support and kindness from friends added layers to my understanding, cultivating this renewed affection within me. The way a friend reached out in support, or how a simple act of kindness could light up my day—each of these moments added layers to my understanding, feeding the roots of this renewed affection. As I learned and let love unfold, I began to realize that culture plays a role in how we love.

I learned to slow down. It seems that in Brazil, the flow of romance carries its unique rhythms—rich, unhurried, allowing love to take root and flourish at its own pace. This cultural perspective contrasted sharply with my initial desire for love to unfold quickly, eager to establish something fulfilling and certain. Yet, my partner taught me the beauty of patience, showing me how to nurture a relationship with attentiveness and calm, letting it grow naturally under the warmth of the Brazilian sun. Through this, I learned to embrace the journey rather than rush to the destination, finding joy in watching our love develop into something both profound and enduring.

With each passing day, this rediscovered love evolved, branching out into every part of my life. It taught me the value of resilience—how love tested and tempered by time becomes not just an emotion but a state of being. I learned to let go of fear and open myself up to love's imperfections, accepting that it's the imperfections that make it genuinely beautiful. With hearts full of hope and love, we decided to spend the rest of our lives together. The decision for him to move to the USA and unite our lives in marriage was exhilarating—a commitment that carried the promise of shared dreams and mutual growth. This journey across borders symbolized more than just a physical move; it was a testament to the powerful bond that sparked from a single online encounter and blossomed into a lifelong partnership.

As we planned our future, a profound sense of belonging and anticipation filled the air, knowing that together we were embarking on a new chapter of unconditional love and support. This journey has not been without its challenges, but each hardship only served to strengthen my resolve. The immigration process would prove to be challenging. We even acquired an immigration attorney to do the legal hard work, which proved key. After almost two years of waiting, my future husband would be landing in Seattle, and our face-to-face relationship would begin. Through this process, I discovered that the essence of love lies in its capacity to renew itself, echoing life's cyclical nature.

Marrying someone from a different country and culture has been one of the most enriching and challenging experiences of my life. Initially, the allure of a new culture was deeply enticing; the language, the traditions, the food—it all seemed vibrant and full of life. However, as the relationship deepened, I began to understand that these differences required navigating a myriad of complexities, far beyond learning a few phrases in a new language or adapting to culinary tastes. The real challenge was finding common ground in our differing cultural norms. Our differing perceptions of family roles, the subtleties in our communication styles, and even the small, everyday habits that were second nature to each of us highlighted the nuances that come with a multicultural union.

These differences initially felt like hurdles, yet they gradually turned into points of growth and mutual understanding. We learned to create a shared culture in our own home, one that respected both his traditions and mine while forging new customs together. It was a

deliberate act of negotiation and compromise, where we let go of certain individual expectations in favor of embracing our joint journey. This process fostered an incredible depth of empathy and a more profound love that transcended our cultural barriers. Despite the challenges, the rewards of overcoming these cultural divides were immense. The experience forged a partnership that is resilient, adaptable, and open-minded, teaching me invaluable lessons about acceptance and building bridges across differences.

Our marriage became a testament to the beautiful complexity of love—one that thrives amidst diversity and flourishes with respect and understanding. It was a quiet evening in August, in the warm glow of our pastor's dining room, surrounded by love and simplicity, when he spoke the words that bound us together—spiritually and legally. As we exchanged our vows, my heart swelled with gratitude and disbelief. For the first time in my life, I felt fully seen and fully loved for who I am. I will never forget that moment and will cherish those special thoughts.

Discovering life together as a gay couple has been an adventure of continuous growth and discovery. From the moment we decided to share our lives, I knew we were stepping into a world filled with possibilities and challenges alike.

Every day is a journey—a unique blend of ordinary tasks and extraordinary moments that remind us of the bond we share. In the early days, it was all new and overwhelming. Learning each other's habits, likes, and dislikes was like unwrapping a never-ending gift. From deciding who takes out the trash to choosing who will make the morning coffee—however mundane—became a quiet act of partnership. These small routines, strung together, formed a rhythm of our shared life, reminding me that love is in the details of every day.

Yet, beyond these everyday routines, we are constantly discovering life on a deeper, shared level. We explore new places, try new foods, and support each other's ambitions and dreams. As a gay couple, fostering an environment where we both feel understood and appreciated has been at the core of our journey. We learn to navigate social perceptions and support each other in the face of obstacles. Each supportive gesture, whether it's holding hands in public or introducing each other to family and friends, is a testament to our love's resilience.

My partner (Vinicius) and I strive to construct a life that is genuinely ours—a matrix of shared experiences and individual growth. Being a part of this beautiful journey fills me with gratitude. Life, with all its unpredictability, becomes a shared canvas where we paint our narrative, one decision and one discovery at a time. The journey is not just about getting through life but about thriving and finding joy in the collective life we are building together.

As my retirement approached, we began dreaming of our future, envisioning a shared life in Brazil. It wasn't just about moving; it symbolized a future shaped by the love we built together—a geographic, emotional, and spiritual home.

CHAPTER 12

LEAVING THE PAST BEHIND

We invested much time and resources traveling back and forth to visit Vinicius's family, embracing the cultural richness and familial ties. When you marry a Brazilian, you marry the entire family. I read this once, and it couldn't have been more true for me. Every trip to visit Vinicius's relatives deepened my understanding of love in Brazil—not just as a bond between two people, but as a whole community of connection and support that wrapped around us. Support that would enrich my life in Brazil and broaden my understanding of family. Our family was wider than our union. I admit I was excited for the possibility of such a dramatic move. First and foremost was the idea of downsizing my life and possessions. Selling the condo marked the first step in our transition, serving as a cornerstone for our financial plans. The proceeds fueled our dream of what lay ahead, providing stability and room to maneuver as we looked toward the next chapter. Next, we decided to give the Prius, a gesture of goodwill as we streamlined our lives. Carefully, we evaluated what would be essential in our new home and made decisions on what we wanted to ship with us. We both were beginning to feel we had made the right decision. The school district granted me four months of salary if I took it off, giving me time to sell, sell, sell. Vinicius was a whiz at packing and wrapping things up. All the larger possessions were out of the question to ship. We chose small things and began each free moment boxing and packing. I spent the day online selling everything else, and the rooms were starting to look bare. This experience made me think: we all carry more than we need. As I sorted through dozens of shoes and suits and all my wardrobe, I realized I would never wear them again. I realized I wasn't just downsizing my closet; I was shedding layers of an identity that no longer fit. This process of sorting made me confront the fundamental question: "What do I truly need?" With that clarity, I decided to streamline my life, clearing out what was not essential, and embraced the vibrant, simplistic lifestyle that awaited me in a new, warmer world. Saying goodbye was harder than I had imagined. As I hugged my friends and family one last time, a mix of emotions swirled within me—a cocktail of sadness and excitement, fear and hope. Each farewell felt like shedding a layer of my old life, poignant and painful yet necessary for growth. I was leaving behind not just people and places, but also parts of myself that no longer served who I wanted to become. Leaving the past behind was like trying to step out of shadow while carrying its weight on my back. I had hoped for a clean break, but life doesn't work that way. The shadows traveled with me, reshaped into lessons, scars, and quiet reminders of where I had been in this journey called life. The emotional weight was palpable, invisible baggage accompanying me with every step. It felt as though I was dismantling a part of my identity, unraveling the threads that stitched together the fabric of my past. Was I ready? Fears and doubts waltzed relentlessly in my mind, taunting me with "what ifs" and "should haves." I often wondered, what if I found myself lost, unable to anchor amid the uncharted seas of my own choosing? Reflecting on the moment I decided to leave my past behind, it feels like running my fingers over a well-loved, well-worn book, marking the close of a significant chapter. It's essential for me to acknowledge that one never truly leaves their past behind. The past remains a part of me, much like running my fingers over a well-loved, worn chapter of a favorite book. Each touch serves as a tangible reminder of the experiences that have shaped my journey. The decision felt like tearing away from a version of myself I'd known for so long. Each part of my life held memories— habits, faces, routines—making the process deeply painful; this decision was not easy. But there was a restless whisper inside me, urging that it was time to move on, time to seek something more, something unknown. Of course, I underestimated how hard it would be to live in a new culture. In my dreams, Brazil is a tropical paradise, yet in reality, it is a country grappling with developmental challenges and a high poverty rate. This duality shapes my perception, balancing the idyllic vision with the complexities I've come to understand. Movers had come, and we made a partial load to be shipped to Brazil, which would take months and a ton of paperwork and emails. We would take a week to explore Canada before we boarded a plane for our new venture. Yet, being in a new relationship, a partnership amid the cacophony, a quiet voice of courage persisted, urging me forward. One day I woke up and realized there was no turning back; I had no home to my name. With each passing day, the old realities slipped further into the shadows. I began to unearth new facets of myself with a partner—one braver and bolder than the last life I lived in theU.S. Boarding the plane, my heart was pounding with anticipation and anxiety. The hum of the engines echoed the tremor of new beginnings. As we took off, I watched the familiar landscapes of my past fade into the horizon, replaced by the infinite possibilities of a new horizon. Arriving in a new country was like stepping onto an unpainted canvas—exhilarating and terrifying in its blankness. The first days were a dizzying blur of sounds and sights, an overload of new experiences. Everything was different—the language, the customs, the air itself. Navigating a culture entirely unlike my own was an adventure in itself. Each day, I found myself learning—learning to understand, to adapt, to belong. It would take a long time to carve out a space for myself, trying to establish new routines and forge connections. It continues to this day that bit by bit, the unknown transformed into the familiar, and the foreign became home. Leaving the past behind was like attempting to step out of shadow while carrying its weight on my back. I hoped that moving forward would mean closure—a chance to embark on a fresh chapter free from all those earlier issues I was dealing with. Yet, as I set forth, I realized those fragments of the past were not easily discarded; they had merely transformed into luggage I carried with me. Each decision I made was influenced by experiences I thought I had outgrown. I wrestled with old insecurities that crept in unannounced, whispering doubts just as I began to feel grounded. It became clear that solving one problem often leads to the emergence of another, reshaping itself into new challenges knitted from the fabric of my history. Acknowledging this was not an admission of defeat but an acceptance that healing does not occur in isolation from the past. Instead, it involves understanding how to navigate life with these remnants, finding ways to grow despite them and sometimes even because of them. Unpacking these emotional suitcases piece by piece has taught me that life is not just about moving forward heedlessly, but about reconciling with the echoes of what once was, crafting a new story where every shadow has its light. Brazil would be the backdrop for this new reality. I was delighted to be so close to the ocean and walk on the warm sand whenever I wanted.

CHAPTER 13

❖────────────❖

NEW FOUNDATIONS BEING BUILT

Moving to Brazil was a profound shift. Nestled within its vibrant culture, I found a chance to explore my true self. The language barrier was one of my biggest challenges; Brazilians speak Portuguese, not Spanish, which made daily life a struggle. Yet, even amidst these struggles, I began weaving a tapestry of experiences that I could call my own. Building an authentic life was more than adjusting to a new routine; it was about dismantling old barriers and reexamining beliefs I once accepted without question. Immersed in Brazil's rhythm, I saw a chance to redefine myself. For the first time, I wasn't just living—I was living as me. Almost like being born again. A gay man. A married man. A man finally fully seen for my true self. This transformation was not without its struggles. There were moments of doubt, of longing for familiarity, but I saw them as parts of my journey rather than obstacles. Brazil's vibrant energy forced me to question and confront the narratives I had carried with me—what did success mean? How did freedom look and feel? Gradually, the answers came not through contemplation alone, but through living; through dancing to samba in the streets, through dining with neighbors who quickly turned into friends, and through the deliberate act of listening and learning from a culture so generously open, spirited and rich with music. Embarking on this path of authenticity was a series of steps— sometimes forward, sometimes back. Yet, with each step, I moved closer to a life that felt genuinely fulfilling. The lessons I encountered here—about embracing ambiguity and finding clarity within chaos—helped shape my narrative, allowing me to build a life that was not just about existing, but thriving wholeheartedly.

One of the most challenging aspects was trying to confront the language barrier. Daily life without a command of the Portuguese language meant that each interaction was a test. It pushed me to rely not just on words, but on gestures, smiles, and an openness that transcends linguistic limitations. Every conversation in Brazil required patience and humility. I relied on gestures, smiles, and openness to communicate. Despite their shyness, Brazilians often showed exceptional kindness—complete strangers would approach me, offering, "Do you need some help? I speak more or less English." The term "gringo," which I initially feared as derogatory, turned out to be a casual and welcoming expression.

Vinicius and I made a significant decision—we chose a large high-rise condo in the capital city, João Pessoa of Paraíba, sitting less than a mile from the enchanting ocean. This was not just a mere relocation; it was a leap into our life built together. Investing my retirement into this home felt monumental, but more than that, it signified our commitment to building something real, long-lasting, and shared. This decision was not taken lightly. To

Investing everything that I had saved over my career into this new abode required us to be sure that this was where we wanted to build our future. As we stood looking at the magnificent view, the vast ocean spreading out below us, it felt as if the world was opening up, inviting us into a future filled with endless possibilities. The choice of this condo as our foundation symbolizes our leap into a life of authenticity, rooted in the vibrant culture and welcoming community of Brazil.

The process of settling in was a test of resilience and adaptability, as we navigated this new world, embracing a lifestyle so rich and different from what we had known. Here, in this flourishing city, we pledged to discover the rhythm of life, to broaden our horizons, and most significantly, to grow together.

João Pessoa is a city that truly captivates with its blend of natural beauty and vibrant urban life. As I wander through its streets, I am taken by the unique mix of old-world charm and modern flair. The city is alive with color, from the pastel hues of colonial-era buildings to the bright outfits of people bustling about. It feels like each corner tells a story, inviting me to be part of its tapestry. The ocean's proximity brings a soul-soothing calm, with the beach serving as a daily escape from life's hustle. Walking along the shore feels indescribable— watching surfers glide across the waves while the sun sets in a blaze of color. The salty breeze gently embraces me, making my worries drift away, leaving peace in its place. João Pessoa is not just about beautiful landscapes; it's about the warm embrace of its people and the rich culture that thrums through the city. Street markets and small cafes provide glimpses into everyday life, where the aroma of freshly brewed coffee mingles with the laughter of people. It's in these vibrant interactions that I find myself discovering not just a new city, but a new way of life.

Adaptation is a constant theme here, pushing me to embrace changes and appreciate the richness of living in this remarkable corner of the world. This journey taught me that authenticity is messy, non-linear, and sometimes exhausting. But it's also exhilarating. Each stumble brought me closer to a life that was not just tolerable, but deeply fulfilling, rooted in truth and courage.

CHAPTER 14

BUILDING AN AUTHENTIC LIFE

After most of my life spent hiding my orientation, the move to João Pessoa felt like a lighthouse of hope, a chance to construct the life I always envisioned but had never fully grasped. Here, in the rhythm of a new city and surrounded by ocean breezes that whispered freedom, I was finally able to live authentically. I realized that telling the truth wasn't just about uttering words; it was about living those words, embracing each piece of my identity without apology or fear. Yes, telling the truth takes practice. It's one thing to say who you are—it's another to embody it daily, in conversations, in relationships, in how you carry yourself through the world. I was used to hiding and telling untruths at all costs. This journey wasn't about forcing the past into obscurity; rather, it involved integrating it into the vibrant mosaic of my new experiences. Learning to be real instead of donning a façade had its challenges, but each step brought me closer to a profound liberation. I was unlearning years of pretense, allowing my genuine self to flourish in this supportive, colorful environment.

Living my truth meant reconciling with my past while investing in a future built on authenticity and courage. João Pessoa, with its breathtaking vistas and welcoming ambiance, became the backdrop of a transformative chapter where

I could explore, connect, and express myself fully. The freedom to live openly as a gay individual in this vibrant culture wasn't just a change of location—it was the dawn of an entirely new life. This evolution teaches me that even as we carry remnants of our old lives with us, there is incredible power in choosing to define ourselves anew, every day. As I embraced my new life, I also began to observe how the broader gay culture interacted with the overall culture of Brazil. In Brazil, gay people enjoy a fairly open environment, but it's not something often talked about within the immediate family. This is a culture that is full of shame, mainly brought by the religious establishment. It is much like the USA, with the evangelical church causing judgment and pain to all individuals. To my delight, Vinicius and I can walk down the streets holding hands or putting his arm around me as we walk. I never dreamed of such a scene. Building an authentic life together, after years spent in hiding and shame, has been a journey of both liberation and uncertainty. Most of my life was shadowed by fear—fear of rejection, fear of being misunderstood. But stepping into a life of openness with my partner marks a turning point that is as exhilarating as it is daunting.

For instance, even now, when someone glances too long as we hold hands, I feel that old tension rise in my chest—the instinct to hide or pull away. But I don't. It quickly became apparent that the remnants of my old life still lingered. The shame, though lessened, occasionally surfaced, reminding me of the years spent in secrecy. Embracing authenticity requires us to confront these shadows with courage and understanding. Together, Vinicius and I have learned to navigate the complexities of building a life that is truly ours. We've had to redefine what love means in the context of honesty and vulnerability. This relationship isn't just about sharing a home; it's about sharing truths, fears, and dreams— each revelation another brick in the foundation of a life built on authenticity. This relationship isn't just about sharing a home; it's about laying a foundation. Every truth we speak, every fear we name, and every dream we share becomes another brick in the life we are building. Authenticity, like a well-built house, requires patience, care, and trust. While the past may have shaped us, it no longer holds the pen. Together, we're writing a new story, one where authenticity outshines shame and where love, finally free, leads us forward. It challenges us to continuously redefine ourselves and our place in the world.

CHAPTER 15

THE RIPPLE EFFECT

With the unwavering support of my partner, I've experienced not only personal transformation but also witnessed our relationship become a source of inspiration and connection for many in our community and extended family. In Brazil, family is a fundamental pillar, even more deeply ingrained than I experienced in the USA. It's family first, and I've embraced this wholeheartedly. Moving to Brazil meant merging into Vinicius' entire family dynamic. As our family connection deepened, so did our desire to give back. Living and working in the USA gave Vinicius and me a significant economic advantage when we moved back to Brazil. In Brazil, family extends beyond the immediate; it's about everyone who shares in your life, in all its vibrant, chaotic, and beautiful forms. Each gathering deepened my immersion into their culture. They welcomed me with warmth and an intensity that was both overwhelming and heartwarming. Every event was alive with laughter, music, and sometimes intense debates, where I learned that family ties here reach into every facet of life. From helping a cousin in need to hosting a spontaneous visit from a distant relative, marrying into a Brazilian family meant embracing a vast interconnected community. This realization,initially daunting, became a comforting reminder of the family bond's strength, turning challenges into cherished memories. In Brazil, I've come to realize that unity in diversity isn't just a concept; it's a way of living, loving, and growing together. Thanks to the opportunities that arose, we have witnessed substantial improvements in the quality of life for our loved ones—aspirations that once seemed unreachable in the USA became reality. Our financial stability allowed us to contribute to projects and support educational goals, turning dreams into tangible achievements. This empowerment strengthened our familial bonds and added depth to every investment. As you consider the power of economic changes, remember how they can directly enrich personal lives, making aspirations tangible and deeply meaningful.

Moving to Brazil and fully living an authentic life not only transformed my world but also sent ripples across the lives of my two sons and friends who stayed behind in the USA. It's as if my newfound freedom and honesty became a silent ambassador of change, inspiring them in ways I hadn't expected. Seeing me live openly and with conviction has profoundly impacted my sons, challenging them to reconsider their perspectives on authenticity and courage. I believe it has encouraged them to examine their lives through the lens of honesty, showing that living truthfully can lead to a fulfilling existence. This transition subtly invites them to explore their own definitions of happiness and self-expression.

Now, as a grandfather, it's difficult not being able to see them grow up. I miss the chance to hold them, to read them bedtime stories, and just to be present as they grow. Still, I hope that one day, these ripples of authenticity might bring us closer in ways I can't yet see. I moved to Brazil and started a new life with my Brazilian partner. It's a life I've built with care, full of love and daily moments. But even here, beneath the warmth of this new chapter, there's a quiet, constant truth: I'm still a father. It's hard to put into words what it feels like to be a father from a distance—a father in name, but not in the day-to-day lives of my sons. They're back in the United States, living their lives, growing up, and becoming who they are meant to be. But I'm not there. I don't hear their voices. We don't have real conversations. There are no holiday gatherings, no birthday celebrations, no moments to mark time together. I see them only through the screen—snippets of their lives shared online. Photos.

Posts. Moments I wasn't part of. And while I'm grateful to catch even a glimpse, it breaks something inside me every time. I long to be more than a spectator. I ache to be their dad in the real sense—in the way that matters most. But instead, I exist on the edges, like a ghost hovering near the life I should be part of. The silence between us is heavy. Some days, it's unbearable. And in the quiet, I find myself asking: what does it mean to be a father when your children live without you? They're living their lives, becoming who they are meant to be. And I watch from afar, silently cheering for them, loving them from a distance they may never feel.

Similarly, my friends back home have noticed the change from afar. It's sparked introspection among them about societal norms we grew up with. Some admire my journey and share their own stories, inspired by my choice to embrace authenticity. Yet, for some reason, visits to Brazil from them remain an idea never quite realized. While most of my friends connect with me only online now, those rare messages and shared memories still carry meaning—reminders that some connections, even distant ones, continue to ripple through our lives. In these ways, the decision to live openly in Brazil, embracing my authentic self, has resonated beyond borders. It's evident that the internal revolutions we undertake don't stay contained within us; they ripple outward, touching the lives of those we care about and sometimes challenging their own paths towards authenticity and acceptance.

In this time, I've come to cherish my own company—learning to befriend the quiet within. In solitude, I've found serenity, where each mindful breath reveals life's quiet beauty. This inward peace, too, ripples outward, shaping how I show up for others—with presence, with gratitude, and with grace. Embracing a new chapter in my life, I realized the importance of self-care and tending to my needs in this beautiful world I live in. As I learned to befriend myself, I discovered that it's okay to pamper and prioritize my well-being. This journey has been about finding balance between nurturing my spirit and embracing the small, exquisite moments that offer joy and fulfillment. All my life, I believed that taking care of myself was selfish. Now, I've embraced the importance of it. This inward peace ripples outward, shaping my interactions with others—with presence, gratitude, and grace. I learned to pamper and prioritize my well-being, finding balance in nurturing my spirit and cherishing the small, exquisite moments each day offers. Embracing my needs has become about living with fulfillment and authenticity.

CHAPTER 16

✦————✦

THE JOURNEY OF ACCEPTANCE AND PEACE... NO SECRETS KEPT

As I wrap up these memoirs, I find myself not at the end but standing at the edge of something still unfolding. Moving to Brazil and living openly has brought me to a place of peace I once only dreamed of. The freedom to be fully myself has replaced years of hiding with wholeness, and yet, the journey continues—each day a new page, a new learning, and each moment another step toward a deeper understanding. Yet, the journey is far from over. Each day is a new chapter filled with lessons and insights too numerous to mention in one sitting. Living here has taught me that life is a continuous process of learning and growing, each experience building upon the last. The delight of new friendships, the love felt within a supportive community, and the revelations about my own strength and resilience have been invaluable as I continue to build a life reflective of my true self. Embracing this path was not just a decision to seek happiness but a commitment to living a life enriched with authenticity and courage. It is with gratitude that I look forward to the future, knowing that the journey of self-discovery and acceptance promises new horizons and endless opportunities for growth. As I write this final chapter, I am celebrating another year. In Brazil, we call it aniversário! How amazing to think of life as an anniversary. Many here ask, "How many years do you have?" Living in Brazil has introduced me to a different way of celebrating life. Here, I've realized that anniversaries often hold more significance than birthdays. Brazilians have a unique way of cherishing milestones that encompass not just individual progress but shared experiences that strengthen family bonds. The custom is less about aging and more about commemorating the journeys we've taken together, marking the passages of time through the connections we've deepened. This shift in perspective has taught me to value the collective moments we've built—celebrations that acknowledge not only personal growth but the growth of our relationships and community. It's a beautiful reminder that life is a continuous narrative of shared stories and that every additional year is a testament to the journey we've undertaken together. Today is filled with constant interruptions and visitors just dropping by— what a life. When you think you've learned all there is, life offers a new challenge. Facing heart surgery in a foreign country feels daunting and unexpected. Much like coming out, facing surgery stripped me bare— physically and emotionally. It was another moment of surrender, and in that surrender, I found surprising strength and amazing loving supportive care. I underwent successful open-heart surgery with a profound reminder of life's fragility. I spent two weeks in intensive care and medical follow-up with no price tag. This experience marked a pivotal moment in my journey, teaching me the invaluable lesson of gratitude for each heartbeat. The surgery was an emotional wake-up call that reinforced the transient nature of existence, and it pushed me to reassess my priorities and how I wanted to spend the remainder of my life. Emerging from such a critical operation with renewed vigor, I found myself deeply inspired.

It became clear that my story was not over but had just begun to take a different shape. The physical challenges I faced during recovery revealed my resilience and ignited a passion to live each day fully. I've come to view each sunrise as a canvas filled with untapped potential, and every interaction as an opportunity to forge deeper connections, both with others and within myself. As I journey forward, I carry with me a deeper appreciation for the simple joys that life offers—be it a heartfelt conversation, a moment of stillness by the ocean, or the vibrant colors of a Brazilian sunset. These experiences remind me that while life is indeed fragile, it is also beautifully resilient, and it's this resilience that allows my narrative to continue unfolding with acceptance and peace. Now each sunrise becomes a blank canvas, and I—the artist—am no longer painting with fear but with bold colors of joy, honesty, and grace. As I conclude this memoir journey, I want to reflect on the new insights and lessons I've gained about living authentically. Life's path has taught me to embrace change with open arms and find peace in the uncertainty of each step. This journey has shown me the importance of understanding and accepting my true self, particularly in reconciling my faith and identity and embracing the love and support of my partner and community. As I age, I notice my view on life evolving. What once seemed crucial no longer holds such weight. Peace, happiness, and love have become far more important than drama, stress, or the urge to impress others. Life has taught me that time is precious, and I now see that as I age, I've embraced choosing peace and letting go of the noise around me. I've learned to be thankful for what I have, to love deeply, live simply, and savor moments that truly matter, each day as a true gift. As you age, you learn to cherish the small things— a hot cup of café, a quiet evening, a loving hug, or laughter with close friends. A cozy home, simple meals, and genuine company become the greatest blessings. I've learned that resilience and courage blossom in adversity, and the beauty of connection and community enhances the human experience. Each chapter of my life has contributed to a deeper understanding of who I am and who I strive to be—embracing every moment and interaction, no matter how small, as an opportunity for growth and reflection. Living authentically, I have found strength in vulnerability and solace in the clarity of self awareness. With every breath, I'm reminded that resilience is the quiet thread holding it all together. And so, the journey for me continues—with acceptance, with peace, and with no secrets left to hide.

SOME FINAL THOUGHTS

This memoir is a testament to the journey of becoming. My hope is that in these pages, readers find reflections of their own struggles and triumphs—and that they feel empowered to step fully into their truth. As I step into this next chapter of life, I've distilled the insights I've gained into what I jokingly call my 10 commandments—but they're really more realizations, hard-won through years of searching and surrender. I have called them my 10 commandments, but they are more like REALIZATIONS:

I. Find Peace in Something Bigger than YOU

Embrace the divine within and around you. Distinguish spirituality from mere religious routine, anchoring your soul in something transcendent and meaningful. Walk to the mighty powerful ocean.

II. Live Generously and Give Freely

Liberate yourself from the chains of materialism. Serve the poor with humility, and remember that true wealth is in giving freely. Loosen the grip of 'more'.

III. Nurture Your Physical Temple—BODY

Treat your body as the magnificent vessel it is. Fuel it with nourishing foods and drinks, ensuring it's well cared for as you navigate life's waves. Resist the passivity that can creep in with age or comfort.

IV. Embrace the Present Moment

Release the grip of past regrets and future anxieties. Focus on the now, where life's richness truly unfolds in each heartbeat. Don't worry about tomorrow! Embrace change.

V. Prioritize Relationships

Build bridges of love and friendship. Listen with intention, talk with sincerity, and be the friend who lifts others up simply by being present. Be known as a person of truth.

VI. Keep Moving Forward

Resist the passivity that comes with age. Allow the rhythm of life to be marked by constant movement, whether it's a simple walk or a grand adventure.

VII. Seek Knowledge Daily

Ignite your curiosity and exercise and stretch your mind. Let each day whisper a new insight, deepening your understanding of the world and yourself. Try to learn something new daily.

VIII. Awake with Gratitude

Let dawn break on a heart full of thankfulness. Proclaim aloud the blessings you hold, for this practice wields transformative power. Another day to start anew.

IX. Cultivate Forgiveness

Free your spirit from the weight of grudges. Practice forgiveness and self-kindness, making room for healing and compassion to flourish. Be the first to say 'I'm sorry.'

X. Live Authentically with Passion

Chase after what sets your soul on fire. Be true to your essence, live honestly, and embrace every opportunity to dance in the authenticity of your own truth. Be on guard of your thoughts.

Infuse these commandments with your unique experiences, allowing them to guide and inspire you on your personal journey. May these truths be yours, the ones we shape ourselves. May you walk forward with courage, compassion, and no secrets left to keep.

ABOUT THE AUTHOR

Ken Wortley is a prolific writer in the self-help genre, known for his insightful reflections on personal growth and transformation. With a journey that began eight years ago through journaling, Ken's introspective writings evolved into a collection of thoughtful books. Three years ago, he embarked on writing his memoirs, capturing the essence of his life's experiences. A former pastor with 20 years of service across various churches in the USA, Ken brings depth and compassion to his work. Additionally, his experience as a middle school Language Arts and Social Studies teacher adds a unique educational perspective to his writing. Currently, Ken is engaged in completing his memoirs, aiming to inspire readers with stories of resilience and faith.

www.ingramcontent.com/pod-product-compliance
Lightning Source LLC
Chambersburg PA
CBHW071534120626
46550CB00006B/2461